Bogtrotter
Notes from a North Country cabin

Richard A. Coffey

Acknowledgements

My thanks to the many who have helped make this little book possible during the last thirty-two years. It was my wife, Jeanne, who suggested that a book about our experience be written and who cheerfully maintained order while I cluttered our one-room cabin with typewritten pages. Jeanne read my work and made corrections, she fed the woodstove on many cold January mornings, and at midday she lured me from my corner with fresh baked bread.

It was Bill Swanson, a long-time writer, editor and dear friend that gave this book its life breath thirty years ago, and again in 1996 when he edited the second edition. I thank Paul and Marie Jensen, now sadly passed, of Northfield, Minnesota, who not only introduced Jeanne and me to the wonders of the bog, but checked my manuscript for accuracy.

I certainly thank the people of Hinckley, Minnesota, for preserving the history of the Hinckley fire of 1894, for it was that history that gave much meaning to our adventure—and last, but far from least, I thank our bogland neighbors for their patience, generosity, wisdom, enthusiasm and many memorable delicious family meals on cold winter days.

The incidents in this book are real. I have changed the names of our friends to protect their privacy.

For Jeanne

bog.trot.ter n. A person who lives in or frequents bogs.
— The American Heritage Dictionary

Preface

The only time I've visited Dick and Jeanne Coffey in their home on the bog was in 1982. Usually I don't remember reactions to a place fourteen years after the fact, but I strongly recall wishing for a blizzard that day.

If a snowstorm came up suddenly, I reasoned, what could they do with me? Kick me out? Not these folks. They would graciously give me space on a couch, a quilt or two, access to the hundreds of books on the shelves, another cup of coffee at the old oak table, eventually some delicious soup from the top of the wood cookstove, and maybe even fresh-baked bread. The Coffeys could continue our conversation or clam up, I didn't care. I wanted only to stay.

Dave Wood and I were visiting the Coffeys as reporters for the Neighbors section of the *Star Tribune*. Each month, we picked a Minnesota town of fewer than twenty-five-hundred people and spent about three days there, talking to its residents, gathering stories, discovering its appeal, finding out what made it unique. Even in Minnesota, one town is vastly different from the next.

Dave and I relished the trips. Neither of us got our reporting kicks by interviewing the governor in his executive office or buttonholing high-powered business people in their mahogany suites or asking tough questions of legal eagles or homicide cops.

We liked talking with regular people—decent people, chatty people, folks usually not in the news. We enjoyed hearing their stories as we sat around their kitchen tables or in cafes on Minnesota main streets.

When we chose Hinckley as a "Neighbors town," we both wanted to see the Coffeys on their bog that December day. The sixteen-by-twenty- four-foot, one-room cabin that they built for $1,100 was warm and cozy, heated by the wood they cut. They had no electricity or running water. They told us how they used to live in a condo in downtown Minneapolis. They had been into rushing —to work, to cocktail parties, to fancy restaurants.

"We made a lot of money," Dick told us, "but we spent a lot of money. We were spending our lives earning our lives."

So they quit their jobs in March 1980 and went to live near a tamarack swamp outside of Hinckley, an hour-and-a-half north of the Twin Cities. The book you are about to read tells about the changes they experienced during their first year on the bog.

The Coffeys deliberately chose a place that to most people is wasteland. What they found, as Dick put it, was "an incredible diversity of life, a fragile web of wild existence that hadn't been disturbed by man in search of wealth or recreation."

Back in the Twin Cities, they had tried to find pleasure in fine wines and new cars and airplanes and boats, "but it wasn't until we walked this barren, boggy, bushy land that we had a shot of pure joy," Dick said. They found their serenity in the woods Their purpose in life that year, they concluded, was to live simply and watch life on their bog. Their experience lies in this book.

In lovely, vivid language, Dick describes the beauties and realities of their new life: the snowshoes, woodstove, kerosene lamps, and heavy snows; the coyotes, deer, fireflies, mice, and skunks; the grosbeaks, loons, ruffed grouse, sandhill cranes, and chickadees; the summer vegetable garden and the wild cranberries; the fields of bracken fern and expanses of sphagnum moss; the outhouse; the birch and spruce and popple.

Dick chose details and incidents that make their Minnesota bog come alive to readers anywhere. He writes with elegance about a life that wasn't always elegant.

Although their account ends shortly after Ronald Reagan was inaugurated President, the story stays fresh. I recently reread *Bogtrotter* as I sat on my porch one warm July day, iced tea in hand. Dick's writing is so vivid that I could remember how cold my bones can get in a Minnesota winter.

I still use my "Coffey Standard" to value a Minnesota home. I ask myself, "How long would I be content here during a blizzard?" At the Coffeys' little cabin on the bog, the answer was for days and days.

Peg Meier
Minneapolis, Minnesota
July 1996

Introduction

This time it was by night that I saw our place again. I was flying home to Minnesota from eastern Wisconsin where I had spent the day in a business meeting. I was flying my small airplane above the clouds, going home in the moonlight, flying alone through mountains and valleys of luminescent cloud.

I pulled the throttle back and descended into the cloud as you might drive into a bank of fog in a valley on a lone road in the still chill of night. I watched my instruments to maintain myself right-side up with the world and to obtain clarity of my position over the earth; I sank deeply into the cloud that was illuminated by the soft, pale light of the moon. After a few minutes, as I descended, I began to see a smear of electric light projected into the cloud from below.

This vivid earthly light, I judged, came from the spotlights of the casino near Hinckley, and as I emerged from the cloud, down into the strong, clear night, I saw, just ahead, crepuscular rays of moonlight shining on the empty boglands of the Kettle River basin.

My airplane descended toward the flashing beacon of the Sandstone airport, and when I looked down, I saw our place.

It's not our place any longer, but it was, and it was like an old friend who has illuminated your life and given meaning to your day. This place, this cabin on a spit of high ground surrounded by a boggy wetland, was a friend to Jeanne and me as sure as the human friends we had in those days. It was a teacher, and a quiet place that listened when we spoke. This rude cabin of aspen wood, situated in a forest of spindly white birch, weaned us from our dependence on the society of a city where we were raised and brought us into the country where we learned to depend on ourselves.

Like a friend, this cabin, with its woods and bog, was forgiving of our mistakes, our illusions and our prejudices. And like a friend, this place let us keep some of our illusions, too.

When we came from Minneapolis to the bog in the spring of 1980, we drove from the clarity of our past into a cloud of sorts, for we didn't know what we would find ahead. We had built a small frame cabin in the woods east of Hinckley, and had found pleasure there on weekends and during short vacations from our jobs and a downtown condominium.

As we drove from the city to the country in a Volkswagen van stuffed with chairs and books and cooking utensils and clothing, we listened to the news on the radio. In Tehran, sixty-six Americans were being held hostage by Iranian students. There was talk of a fearsome new disease called acquired immune deficiency syndrome, and though only a few cases of this "lifestyle disease" had been reported, experts were predicting hundreds of thousands would die of it. OPEC had raised fuel prices, Chrysler had received a $1.5-billion Congressional bailout. Gold prices had risen to $800 an ounce.

We turned the radio down and talked about chickadees; and while I drove away from the suburban sprawl of the Twin Cities, northbound, Jeanne read passages from the Audubon Field Guide to North American Birds.

Like many Americans at the dawn of the '80s, we were confused and anxious. Our plan was to leave the city and the bad news behind, and establish ourselves in the cabin we'd built. We planned to live without electricity, without a telephone, and without the help of government safety regulations. We were going to strike out on our own and define our own future. What would become of us, we reasoned, would come by our own hand. We would not be held hostage by the country's "malaise." We were going to carve out a simple life and care for it, like a doe for its fawn.

And we did. Jeanne and I had never been so happy as we were those first few years on the bog. We achieved confidence and independence by digging our own well, building an outdoor sauna, and constructing a marvelously efficient outhouse. While the world listened to President Reagan proclaim that America was not in decline, Jeanne and I bathed in the moonlight, and explored our woodlot and bog as children might explore secret rooms in a magical old house. While our leaders announced production of the neutron bomb and planned their Strategic Defense Initiative, Jeanne and I took longer and more frequent walks under the stars, cherishing our small patch of the planet while it was still in one piece.

Our relative isolation on the bog was constructive. We discovered that in a universe of two people, the price of freedom is mutual responsibility. We learned to work for each other, we learned to share. We spent many hours each day gathering wood for the cookstove, pumping water from our shallow well, and gathering wild berries and garden plants; all of this work was then consumed during a single meal. At night we walked deep into the wood or far out onto the bog, where we stopped, sometimes for hours, and simply listened to the voices of the night. Back at the cabin, we read books and listened to radio dramas until the radio's batteries grew so weak the distant world simply faded away. Then we slept.

The clarity of our past was increasingly obscured by the strength of each day's events, and after we had been on the bog for a year, we felt that the trail back to the city, back to our former lives, had disappeared. We felt as though we couldn't go back, that we had changed.

Just as we no longer felt powerless to survive in a world that had become dependent on the mood swings of the Super Powers, we felt less controlled by the economy. If the consensus held that government should provide solace and support for its citizens, we had learned from our experience on the bog that individuals are ultimately accountable for their actions. We'd learned that happiness came when we controlled our day, when we took responsibility for our own lives.

We lived on the bog for five years, and with each passing year we asked ourselves if we would stay another. It was a serious question, for we were growing older and more distant from the work and the work ethic that had defined our life in the city. Although we could live well on the bog for a fraction of the cost of city life, we were sustained only by my writing and by Jeanne's part-time job as director of the Hinckley Fire Museum. We believed that our new-found self-reliance was the foundation of our life, but we were also curious about testing our new-found confidence in the outside world. We felt, moreover, that the clock was running against us, that we either had to pack up and go back to the world as enlightened and productive employees, or create a life for ourselves anew.

One day I discovered that my knees were swelling. Visits to local doctors produced prescriptions for muscle relaxants, but nothing seemed to reduce the swelling. Finally, I sought help at the Mayo Clinic in Rochester. While I was recovering from arthroscopic surgery, adjusting to a prognosis that I had a form of rheumatoid arthritis, a young doctor quizzed me about the way we lived. He seemed particularly interested in our proximity to an area where he was investigating a disease caused by a wood tick. When he learned that we lived in the woods, and that I had in fact experienced a tick bite that produced a rash, he told me I was probably suffering from Lyme disease. Time would tell, and it did. When Jeanne and I returned to the cabin, we spent two months on snowshoes, and my knees didn't bother me a bit. But my hospital stay had shaken our confidence. We were self-sufficient— but only to a point. If either one of us got sick, our woodland lifestyle would never be able to finance the necessary care. We talked more urgently about leaving the bog and returning to the city.

We replayed a return scenario over and over, trying to imagine how we would fit into an office again, or a neighborhood. We had discovered much about ourselves during the years on the bog, but none of what we learned seemed useful to an ordered life in the city. We'd sold out our equity in the system, and we talked about it late into the night, and we finally gave up thinking about it and decided to stay.

Meanwhile, nearby hunting shacks were becoming permanent homes, the county bogland was put up for bids to peat harvesters, our neighbors were petitioning the county to surface the gravel road. The town of Hinckley had developed a freeway destination, which included plans for a theme park and a motel.

Our little patch of bogland seemed more and more vulnerable, and so, we felt, did we. We wanted to document our experience on the bog and leave before its character changed too drastically. I wrote this book, and then one day, when we were in Sandstone, I noticed that the Pine County Courier was looking for an editor. I got the job, and a year later we bought the paper. I began driving from the bog to the office in Sandstone while Jeanne drove to the museum in Hinckley. We'd become commuters again—commuters who lived in a one-room shack with an outdoor privy.

Eventually we bought a small farmstead near Sandstone, and, pressed by our new work schedules to quickly set up a household, moved most of our belongings out of the cabin. We left the cabin without meaning to. We rushed away in haste, intending to return. But we didn't return for several months, and when we did—when we went to the bog one day to close the cabin and say farewell— we found a cold, silent, empty place.

We walked the trails we had cut and stood for a time, as we had in the past, letting the silence speak, but we heard only the wind, and when we drove into the yard, we felt we were strangers.

The enveloping feeling of warmth that we'd experienced there for five years was gone. The deer were gone, the birds were gone. The Franklin ground squirrel wasn't there to sound the alarm. It was as if something terrible had come to the cabin while we were away.

We picked through the remains of our belongings like victims of a tornado, looking for anything that would testify to and explain the change that had come over the place. We picked up the odd book, a garden tool, a wind-tossed sauna towel, looking for signs of life. But there were none.

I looked at my watch and said, "I have to get back to the office." We drove away, stunned, in silence.

Months later, we worried that we had simply sold out, that we'd changed our idea of how to live, and lost the idea that was, for five years, the cabin. The cabin taught a last lesson that day. You can't have it both ways. You can't live in the comfort of the material world and expect to be rewarded by the spiritual abundance of the simple life.

We now had a newspaper, a monthly check, and a hot shower, but we'd lost the friendship of that cabin on the bog.

A few years later we bought a regional flying magazine and moved the operation in with the Courier. We hired an editor for the paper, and I spent the next eight years in small airplanes, providing flight instruction and writing about aviation. Jeanne developed the museum in Hinckley, competing for tourists with one of the many gambling casinos that had sprung up throughout the region.

And tonight Jeanne and I sit on our deck at the farmhouse in Sandstone and watch the shafts of moonlight reach down to the barn, lighting it as if it were a prop on a very large stage. I tell her I saw the cabin in the moonlight when I flew down out of the clouds on my way back home. We sit close in the chilly air and remember what happened to us on the bog. We think of it often, in fact. The memories are warm and exciting, and they take us back to a time when Jeanne and I found the source of our love for each other and the time when we believed that we could live forever outside the force of the common day.

"We can go back there, you know," Jeanne says.

"I think we've got too much to lose," I reply.

"Ha!" she exclaims, laughing in the darkness. "I think you'd better read your book again!"

So I will.

1

I woke suddenly as an avalanche of snow and ice thundered down off the cabin roof. Jeanne hadn't stirred and was still buried deep in our thick winter quilt, so I got up to begin the first day of our new life in the woods by shoveling a path to the woodpile.

The eastern sky was but a faint glow of the day to come, and the still, cold air was invigorating. Chickadees darted about in little bursts of flight to the sunflower seed feeders. An ermine poked his head out of the woodpile and watched me shovel the heavy snow.

Somehow I felt as if we had been living like this all our lives, yet only the week before we were awakened by the alarm clock in our condominium high above Minneapolis streets. I had spent those early morning minutes listening to television reports of world disorder. I shaved in the company of men on the march in Africa; I brushed my teeth as economists forecasted unemployment and a dying dollar. Terrorist attacks accompanied me to the table where Jeanne had prepared our grapefruit and scrambled eggs.

News of murder slipped into my waking being as easily as the smell of buttered toast.

Jeanne and I had always kissed before boarding separate buses to our offices. The din of sirens and the foul winds of diesel smoke and the clattering of a thousand worn heels of the morning workforce drowned out our shouted goodbyes.

Now the birch swayed in the first morning wind. The smell of woodsmoke and a gray puff from the chimney announced Jeanne's preparation of breakfast. On the bog behind the cabin, whitetail deer in single file crossed the frozen hummocks of sphagnum moss. Red squirrels chattered at blue jays and a snowshoe hare froze like a porcelain statue on the trail as I threw another shovelful of wet snow over my shoulder.

We didn't plan on leaving the city; we simply bought a little woodlot and a great deal of bog for weekend retreats. We wanted a place where we could be alone, and when I tramped around the woods with a real estate agent it struck me that a bog was just the place. There was no lake, no spring, no stream. You couldn't snowmobile in the dense brush, and the property was in a game refuge. The birch trees had a fatal disease, the soil was poor, and the hazel nuts had worms. Because it was a bog, it was low and cold all of the time, wet most of the time, and when the sun broke through the morning fog, the rays were stunted by the thick growth of hazel and alder and bracken. We were searching for a place where we could wake up in the morning and wash our faces in rain water and listen to the dew fall to the earth. We were looking for a place that was so quiet, so uninhabited, that if God wanted to talk to us He could whisper. Jeanne and I were looking for a weekend place to unwind; we were not coming to inspect the woods, repair the woods, or take a stand for or against the woods. We wanted a place to listen to the poetry in the trees and feel the texture and breathe the gas of the woods.

The bog was perfect. We bought it and became weekenders, turning left for the low country when the freeway traffic turned right. In great long lines vacationers crawled to their summer cottages, their lakes and streams. We were alone on the road to the bog. Slowly, carefully, we studied the ecology of the woodland, we reviewed the biology of the upside- down world of the bog. We turned the smallest rock and sat chilled in the cold damp night waiting for the call of the barred owl. We watched the snowbound deer yard in the aspen and spruce; we watched the black bear explore our shed and the red-tailed hawk soar the summer skies above. We counted warblers, built houses for the wrens, and waited for the evening grosbeaks to arrive in October.

We played, we huddled against the snowstorms in our fat warm quilt; we ate cranberries, hazel nuts and blueberries, and shook the yellow pollen from cattails for our morning pancakes. And one fall night as we packed our gear down the road to the car to return to the city, under a harvest moon, the coyotes split the cold night air with one piercing shriek. We stopped in our tracks, and in each other's arms we swore to live on this place someday; we swore to plan our way out of the city.

Wanting to leave the city and actually getting out posed two very different kinds of problems. Dreaming about our boggy moors was difficult while we were surrounded by the city and the activity that a city demands of its inhabitants. Yet we knew the bog was there, somewhere north beyond the haze. Getting out meant giving up jobs that had given us the financial freedom to explore the woods, build a small cabin, and buy tools to maintain the place. But what would we do when we cut the city strings? We had to find a livelihood, we had to pay off mortgages and sell everything that wouldn't fit into a sixteen-by-twenty-four-foot one-room cabin.

Luck was with us. A small museum in Hinckley was looking for a curator. The job was seasonal. From May to October we could run the museum, and then spend November through April on the woodlot. The modest income from the museum work would effectively grubstake us through the winter months. If we sold our condominium and arrived on the bog clean of any debt, we could make it. We applied for the job at the museum.

The rural world is electrified, but our cabin is not. Getting out of the city meant getting rid of everything with an electrical cord on it, and used electrical apparatus is harder to give away than a sackful of zucchini squash. A giant toilet-paper box of electrical devices sat in the middle of our living room for weeks, reminding us of our fading relationship with the system. Roasters and toasters, blenders and pots, crocks, lamps and ice crushers; all artifacts that interpreted our participation in the city network, that explained, in part, the life we were abandoning in search of something else. There in a box marked "Chateau Tissue Bath White 2/ply" were the last of our connections, so to speak, to the city.

Getting out meant giving up our city jobs. It was hard to break the news at the office, telling friends— and accounting—that we were leaving. Leaving a job you like, people you like, and a salary that has become a close friend is damn uncomfortable. It was done, however, with less drama than we had guessed, and with the final check pocketed and the farewell party waived, we were unemployed and off to the woods.

Jeanne's woodstove had warmed the cabin to forty degrees. We stood close to the stovepipe and sipped our coffee, deep in thought. It was snowing when we left the city and for two hours the windshield wiper pushed the wet ice around on the window while we chatted excitedly about our new adventure. Jeanne looked into the back of the van from time to time, and I knew she was working out a plan for the interior decoration of the cabin. I was wondering where we were going to put anything in the middle of a March snowstorm.

When we arrived, the driveway was a sea of mud and snow. Carefully we unpacked chairs and tables and boxes of dishes and pushed them into the tiny wooden cabin. The bright red flowered upholstery of the chair that had so recently been a member of a matched set in the city immediately settled down to a quiet mauve and looked quite nice in a room of rough-sawn aspen boards. Soon there wasn't room to walk, and Jeanne began to sort the necessary from the frivolous while I drove the van out to the road before it could freeze into the muck.

As I walked back to the cabin I stopped to listen to this new land of ours. The snow hissed in the trees and although the sounds of the freeway still thumped in the back of my head, I heard the first yelp of a long coyote call. The shrill bark died quickly in the falling snow, but it was welcome enough. We had arrived.

As we warmed our hands by the woodstove, deer came into the clearing east of the cabin. Quickly Jeanne slipped on her Sorel boots and down vest and stepped outside to retrieve the corn that we had brought from the city. The deer watched her closely, but did not move a muscle. Jeanne poured corn from the bag into the pail and started walking to the clearing. One by one the deer stepped back into the woods and waited as she poured out three piles and returned to the cabin. Cautiously, an older doe stepped into the clearing and sniffed the corn. As soon as Jeanne was back in the cabin, the others, a young buck and another doe, walked into the clearing and began eating the corn.

"I want to call that one Sleepy," Jeanne said, pointing to the older doe with its half-closed eyes. "And look at that little buck! He's Nosey!"

The remaining doe was easy to name. She was small and beautiful and had delicate features.

"Pretty," Jeanne said.

"'Pretty' it is," I said as we watched our first deer make themselves at home.

In a couple days there were fewer boxes to climb over. Jeanne had found places to tuck summer clothes, china, and boxes of mementoes, so we began to settle in and enjoy cabin life with incredible ease. Still, it seemed that we were on an extended vacation. We couldn't get it through our heads that this was it, that we had cut ourselves off from the city and were on our own. The day the stovepipe caught on fire we began to understand where we were.

In our haste to get settled into the cabin, I had been collecting any wood that was available to burn in our stoves. Chunks of green birch had smoldered overnight, and when we woke one morning the room smelled like pine tar. I lit a fire as we tried to track down the new scent, and in a second there was great commotion in the stovepipe followed by a bellowing roar that shook the cabin. Jeanne and I stood there looking at each other, and after some time we realized that we had just had a chimney fire—fortunately, a small one.

"If that fire had gotten away from us, the cabin would have burned down," Jeanne said.

I was thinking the same thing and had a cold shiver at the thought of burning the place down after only one month's tenure.

It occurred to us that we were going to have to learn something out here, that although we may not have planned for it, our little cabin on the bog was going to teach us to be self-reliant. There is fifteen miles between our cabin and the volunteer fire department; it is ten miles to a doctor and thirty miles to a major hospital. We could not live as we lived in the city, dependent upon the system to care for our mistakes. Here we would have to live by our wits and learn to view our life as a fragile element in the complex chemistry that was at work around us.

The red squirrels had started a fracas with a couple of blue jays, and the chickadees were infiltrating the evening grosbeak kaffeeklatsch. Redpolls were everywhere on the frozen yard picking up crumbs. A hairy woodpecker and his small look-alike, a downy, had worked out an arrangement near the suet bag. When the sun had finally risen the members of this miniature orchestra settled down and began reducing five pounds of corn and sunflower seed to dust.

The school bus rumbled down the gravel road in the distance, but as we had nothing to put aboard, it did not stop. I brought in an armful of wood, and the cabin temperature reached sixty degrees. In the main this appeared to be a fine way to live. It was a preferable way for Jeanne and me to live because we were forced to focus on the routine chores of life and thus come to appreciate the basics of survival. It was survival that concerned us so much in the city as members of the television news audience. As institutions fell under the attacks of the left wing and threats of reprisals were issued by the right, Jeanne and I found it difficult to find a hand-hold in the tempest. What we needed was confidence in our ability to survive in spite of the system; we needed to develop the talent to feed ourselves from seeds we planted; we needed to be able to heat a home with a fuel that was readily available and prepared by our own hands. We needed self-respect.

Any lifestyle can sponsor some soul-searching and foster self-respect, but we have found the problem in its most lucid state in the woods. In the city we never had the chance to fight a battle whose outcome would prove or disprove our fitness to live by our wits. We simply provided services many generations removed from the sown seed and received compensation to purchase food, shelter, and recreation. We were lost in the system in the city and feeling trapped. On the woodlot we were alone in our efforts to scrape up home and hearth.

Sitting in our cabin on a cold night, warmed by the wood that we cut, filled with the food that we sowed, was a satisfying moment. We were proud of ourselves, respectful of our abilities, and confident in the future. Our reward was the knowledge that we could take care of ourselves, that we could provide for ourselves food, shelter, warmth, and interesting times without television, hamburger stands, parlors, pills, or machines that play ocean sounds at bedtime. What we were to do with this knowledge, whether we lived in the woods or returned to the city one day, mattered not. The lesson would apply anywhere we wanted to live. Once we built the confidence to take care of ourselves, to be pleasant company, the fences would come down. We could go anywhere, survive anywhere, and be anything we wanted to be.

By the end of March we had settled into our new life, cutting wood by day and relaxing sore muscles by the fire at night. We read books that we had always promised ourselves to read and listened to the quiet strings of an FM broadcast on our battery-powered radio. On the night of the spring solstice we put on our

Sorels and, armed with flashlights, went on a tramp in the woods. We set a fire, we dressed in wool, and stepped into the world of pale light and long shadows.

The woodlot was a place of change, a stage of many different plays, each presenting the birth, life, and death of its actors. It was a place of hutches and holes. There was terror for some behind the brush pile, play for many in the clover, and conception in the leaves. The woodlot could be an Elysian dream one moment and a blood-spattered nightmare the next. Winter was pure Brueghel the Elder. Our highland, surrounded by bog, was at once a sanctuary for the frightened and a table for the hungry. It was always coarse and cruel and seldom weighted for the benefit of a single species. It was a place where the weak supported the breath of the strong— a partisan place.

As we moved out onto the trails, through the shadows that shifted in the wind, we interrupted the affairs of a mouse. These were bad times for the mouse. The snow was shallow and hard-packed, the food supply encased, and warm burrows were hard to come by. Tunnels in the snow did not exist. The mouse we startled was caught in the open and used valuable fuel in its panic, a panic that sent her scurrying off to the woodpile, home of the ermine.

We passed the maple tree where earlier in the day we watched a ruffed grouse high in the branches. It was a bad winter for her, too. Feeding on the male aspen buds, she had to wait for warmer temperatures to free the seeds of the ice cases created by a storm earlier that week. The deer were behind us, moving quietly. A single-engine airplane drifted slowly through the night far above. The full moon gave the pilot enough light to see the ragged definition of the no-man's land below. He was high, just a purr of an engine to us, and he could see the lights of Duluth ahead. A twig snapped. There was something on the trail ahead. The deer heard it and stopped moving behind us.

Jeanne and I were the best-equipped but least-able occupants of the trail that night. We continued against the snap of a twig because we believed that it didn't concern us. We had equipped ourselves to know that there was no animal of danger to us. If there had been a threat we would have been the least able to defend ourselves. We could not run like the deer, we could not freeze and melt into the brush like the hare, nor could we fight our way out of a corner like a badger. The snap of another twig stopped us. Stillness enveloped the woodlot. Everyone was waiting. Everyone in the woods that night waited, straining for evidence in the brush. Jeanne's stocking cap was motionless in the moonlight, her breath vaporized and drifted into the trees. Something moved behind us. The tension drained away with time, the hand of the unseen player had been called by the deer, and we moved on.

The deer passed off to our right. They were going to the ridge where they could check our passage out of their territory. Another group of whitetails lived beyond the ridge, and they would be resting just off the trail in the snow. We had seen the rectangular impressions in the melted ice on many hikes before. The old doe of the group heard us long before we gained the ridge. She would monitor our progress with her ears and nose.

A distant wolf call echoed in the cold night air. The old doe snorted, and her group rose on the ready in the brush. We stopped and listened. The wolf would not waste his energy chasing deer that night. He had found a hare or grouse, losers in the moonlight and hard-packed snow. There was a thump in the brush just ahead. A young buck vented his fear, stamping on the frozen boggy earth with a foreleg. The old doe was probably annoyed by his anxiety. Whitetails survive by being quiet. Like the hare and the grouse—unseen, unheard, and able to retreat quickly if discovered.

The winter flocks of chickadees lived behind the ridge in the older forest of rotting aspen. The birds waited out cold nights in the holes of decayed trees, at rest, feathers fluffed, conserving their energy for the cold sunrise flight in search of seed. The males had been exchanging their fee-bee song in preparation for the territorial skirmishes of spring. That night there wasn't a sound, not a hint of the presence of hundreds of birds in the trees.

We turned into a ravine that reflected the full light of the moon. Jeanne stopped and pointed to the ridge. High above us, just a silhouette in the moonlight, a deer moved in the shadows of birch and through a stand of maple. We had reached the limits of another deer yard. Beyond, through the ravine and out onto the bog, is the roughland of the brush wolf. We had seen a coyote once on a night like this, circling, head down, tracking a lone doe. It is seldom that a coyote will bring a deer down, but its presence disturbs the herd and the men who hunt the deer. Coyote dens are sought after in these parts. When they are found, they are unearthed and the pups are shot dead.

The wind returned as we made our way back to the cabin. The first gusts rattled the loose birch bark, a rasping whir, then the upper branches began their slow chant, and the trunk of the birch twisted from its sleep and joined the dance under the full moon. Jeanne and I removed our mittens and held the trunk of a tall, slender, twisting tree. It was cold to the touch, but firm and alive and strong in its movement. There is life in the woods at night, there is vitality in the woody plants and warm blood coursing through the bodies of the animals waiting for food and watching for death.

Yellow light from the cabin windows splashed across the snow and met us on the trail. Jeanne took my hand. All our dreaming and planning had paid off; we were alone in the woods to learn something of simple living, to rediscover our abilities for survival in a world where survival is on everyone's mind.

2

Grab hold of this wire here and walk it on up to your house," the man in the green parka said with a cigar between his teeth. "When you get there, give it a tug three times. Here, you might as well take your phone with you. A black wall phone, right?"

I tucked the phone under my arm and started up our long driveway with the heavy black wire slithering through the mud behind me. In the city it was common to pick up your new telephone at the company's headquarters, but this was the first time I'd picked up the telephone line as well.

"Don't forget to give yourself some extra wire up there," the service man shouted after me. I turned to wave and watched the huge reel unwind as I walked the wire to the cabin. The black line snaked out of the truck and disappeared into the mud of our road. "I'll be there to hook you up in a few minutes," the man shouted.

"What's that?" Jeanne asked as I stumbled into the yard.

"It's our telephone," I said, yanking on the wire three times. A horn sounded on the road, answering my signal.

We hadn't planned on a telephone for our primitive cabin; full appreciation of our isolation seemed to preclude any connections to the system. But signing on with the museum changed all that. A few weeks after we had settled into the cabin we were asked to come into town for a meeting with the full committee about our new job as curators.

It was a wet, sleety March night when Jeanne and I walked into the meeting room of the town library. Waiting for us were nine well-dressed committee men and women. Three of them had interviewed us for the job a few months earlier, the rest were getting their first look at us: a couple of muddy, middle-aged ex-city people dressed in ragged down vests, wet jeans, and rubber boots—with unwashed hair that poked out of our black stocking caps. I put my torn gloves on the table.

"I'd like to introduce our new curators, Dick and Jeanne Coffey," the chairman said. The committee people looked down the table at us, and we smiled at their sober faces.

The meeting was short. We told of our plans to prepare the museum for its opening in May, complimented the group on a fine museum, and asked if there were any questions. They looked at us, they looked at my gloves that had leaked a tiny pool of muddy water on the table. No one had a question.

After the meeting the chairman seemed pleased. "Oh, they know you're living in the woods, I wouldn't worry about that," he said. "But I think you'd better plan to get a phone put in out there. We had an awful time getting word to you that we were having this meeting." He gave us the number of the telephone company, and we promised to get a phone as soon as possible.

We made our call the next morning at the country store. Jeanne placed our order. "All we want is a plain black wall phone," she said. "No, I think one phone will be plenty. Well, our bedroom is in the same room as the kitchen...living room is, too. See, we live in a one-room house...a cabin, actually. Yes, we *are* employed."

Jeanne winked at me as I started down the aisle to do our shopping.

"No, we don't have electricity," Jeanne told the sales representative.

I wondered whether they would let us have a phone at all.

The serviceman plodded up our driveway, but when he came to the yard he stopped, took the cigar out of his mouth, and stared at our cabin. I went outside to see if I might be of some help.

"You living in that?" he said, not taking his eyes off the small gray building.

"Yep," I said proudly, turning to look at the place myself. It wasn't particularly picturesque during the spring thaw. The deck was covered with birch chunks, and chips of bark were scattered about the muddy yard, floating here and there in puddles of water.

"Looks like a hunting cabin," the serviceman said with a sigh, shifting his toolbox from one hand to the other and putting the cigar back between his teeth. "You got electric yet?" he asked as we climbed to the deck and stepped around piles of firewood.

"Naw, we're going to try living without it for a while," I said, hoping to sound like an expert homesteader familiar with the harsh ways of the wilderness.

He looked at me hard and grunted.

Jeanne put the coffee pot on the stove. The man unzipped his parka and looked around at the cabin's interior while he stripped a wire.

"You must have built this yourself," he said finally. He was staring at our ceiling of green aspen boards.

"Yes, it was our weekend cabin," Jeanne said, pouring a cup of coffee for the man. "And now we're living here full-time. Do you use sugar or anything?"

"Black's fine. How long you been here?"

"A month," I said.

He grunted again. "You'll be wanting electric pretty soon. It's okay like this for a while, but they all get tired of it. Wait until this summer when you can't keep your food cool." He smiled at Jeanne and threw a small piece of wire on the floor. "And pretty soon you'll want your TV and indoor plumbing." He looked around.

"You have water?"

"No, we're carrying it from a farm up the road. We get twenty gallons every few days," I said.

"Get a well drilled," he said. "I'm telling you, people don't think about those things until they need 'em. Think they're saving money."

It didn't take him long to tell us about all the people he'd seen come up to the woods from the city. "They come up here to get away from the rat race, okay? Then first thing you know they've never seen a rat race like trying to get wood up for the winter or water outta one of these here shallow wells. It doesn't turn out to be the kinda life they thought, because one day they've up and gone." He leaned into his work and hung the black phone on the wall.

"Well, we've given that some thought," I said.

"They all did," he said, pushing his tools back into the box. "They all come up here like they're the first ones to settle the place. Hell, my grandpa came out here before they had electric, but when they put a line in on that road out there he was the first one to hook up."

We drank our coffee and listened. There wasn't any point in explaining that we had come to the woods to live simply because we wanted to try it. How do you tell a man who has sweated out an existence for his family that you just moved into his country to watch birds and feed deer and write a little poetry on cold winter nights?

After explaining that we'd have to ground our phone by throwing a wire into a puddle of water— "Won't get no ring otherwise"—and assuring us that the telephone company would be back to bury the line and finish the installation when the frost went out, our first visitor left, cigar between his teeth, boots sucking mud. After one last look, he shook his head, and then we heard his truck rumble away.

Jeanne and I stared at the plastic phone on our rough-sawn lumber wall. Three cast-iron frying pans were hanging on nails; two trivets and a salt safe were stationed near the phone that would ring one long and two short and shatter the silence. We were one of eight families on the line, and we envisioned constant ringing. I turned the volume as low as it would go, and we avoided the wall for the rest of the day.

Jeanne began a bread-making project, and I crossed "phone" off the list of work to be done. The next task on the list had been put off since we arrived. I avoided it because of rain, I avoided it because of cold and snow. I didn't get around to it because I didn't have the vaguest notion of what I was doing until Jeanne found a magazine article that gave explicit instructions. On the list it read simply, "outhouse."

While we were weekenders we merely slipped out of the cabin into the night with a flashlight and found an old log where we enjoyed a wilderness "bathroom" under the stars and swaying birch trees. During the winter months it was a speedy trip. Now, as permanent settlers, a real outhouse had to be constructed over a deep, gloomy hole that I had dug the fall before.

Every outside privy we had experienced in the past was dark and smelly and inhabited by insects. We wanted ours to be a cheerful place: bright and exciting, flooded with color and light. We chose a fiberglass roof slanted to the south to catch the warming rays of the low winter sun. The door would have to face north, though we had to wait for our first winter storm to discover the error in that design.

I constructed a wooden foundation over the hole and climbed in from time to time to retrieve fallen tools. I erected the small walls with studding on the exterior so the inside of the place would have few nooks for spiders to build their nests. The plans suggested a toilet-seat height that appeared too high for comfort, so I returned to the cabin to consult with Jeanne.

When I opened the cabin door, the smell of apple pie hit me. "I thought you were baking bread," I said, watching steam rise from the golden crust of the pie on the counter.

"Oh, I thought I would try a pie in case we have more company," Jeanne said. "Maybe we won't look like such beginners if I serve them a fresh pie baked without electricity."

"The telephone man bother you?" I said.

"Haven't you noticed how everyone gets steamed up when they talk about our lack of electricity—I mean it really bothers people, and it isn't even their problem."

"But look who it is," I said. "These are the children of the settlers who came into this country and killed themselves to build roads across the swamps, string electric wires, and get phone service. Most of the people around here grew up living like we are now."

"We're trying to get away from everything they've been trying to achieve," Jeanne said. "Well, one thing that they have that we need is water. I think we'd better go and get some so I can do the dishes. It's bath night tonight, too."

Our water came from a farm several miles up the road. We filled a milk can, a five-gallon pot, and several canteens each time we made the trip. The people who farmed the place were lifelong residents of the county, and as friendly as they were helpful to our adventure. Every visit was a long one over coffee and fresh cake and chatter about the "doings" on the road. More often than not, Ted and Louise offered their good advice about our projects and saved us long journeys down dead-end paths. They accepted our primitive lifestyle, but thought, given time, we'd "go modern."

When we arrived, Jeanne went into the house to talk to Louise while I filled the cans with water from an outside faucet. I loaded the cans into the car and went in and found my place at the kitchen table. Louise was a woman in her early forties, a mother of five; and like most rural women, she could split a cord of wood as easily as she could cook a feast for twelve people. She was always in good humor and was telling Jeanne about something Ted had been up to that morning. The house was warm and smelled of fresh chocolate cake and coffee. It was a smell that was as much a part of their home as was their laughter and love for each other. The kitchen was the center of all activity. It was there that Jeanne and I learned to play whist, learned to sharpen an axe, and listened to tales of wolves and bear and bobcat. I was basking in those memories when I remembered the outhouse.

"Louise, could I borrow a yardstick?" I said.

"Sure." She got up from the table and rummaged around in the closet. She gave me the yardstick, and I went into the bathroom. "Where's he going with that?" she asked Jeanne.

The toilet was fifteen inches high. I tried it for size and returned to the kitchen. "Jeanne, come here a minute," I said. "Go into the bathroom and see if the seat is the right height for our outhouse."

"What?"

"Just do it," I said, pushing her along.

"Is everything okay in there?" Louise shouted from the kitchen.

"Just fine," I answered. "We're just measuring your toilet."

"Never had our toilet measured before," Louise said when we returned. "What's up?"

I explained my construction problem. By that time Ted had joined us. He argued for a low model, Louise for a higher one.

"It isn't going to do you any good if you can't get up on the thing," Ted said.

"You ever tried to get off one that's built too low?" Louise asked.

We all agreed that when it was forty below zero an inch or two either way wouldn't make much difference, so Jeanne and I left to finish our work before dark.

For the rest of the day I hammered away on the outhouse while Jeanne cleaned the cabin. Shortly before sunset I invited her up the hill to inspect my work.

"It's super," she said, stepping into the tiny cubicle. The wind picked up and the fiberglass roof rattled. "We'll paint it white inside, and I have that Dürer print for this wall," she said.

"Look at that view," I said, facing the north in front of the door. "Miles of birch and bog to look at...."

"If you leave the door open," Jeanne said.

"What's the difference out here?" I said. "We're alone."

In the distance a ruffed grouse was drumming its mating call on a log. The last rays of sunlight spread across the bog, and the texture of acres of sphagnum moss was vivid, framed by the tall birch. Purple finches were everywhere chirping, while a red-winged blackbird called to the setting sun with a loud, clear o-ka-leeee.

A chattering sound came from the cabin. Then another. "The telephone," Jeanne said, and we ran down the path to see if it was our ring. When we got to the deck we saw a deer at the corn pile. She had heard the ring, too, and her great ears were raised as she listened while the phone chattered out another refrain: three short and one long. That wasn't us. In a few minutes the ringing stopped, and silence rushed in to fill the void. The grouse drummed, and the deer chewed loudly on the corn.

"I don't think I'm going to like having a phone," Jeanne said. "I don't feel far away anymore."

I didn't, either. The outside world had gained entry to our retreat. The busy gossip of society had turned from the country road and followed the long black wire into our cabin. Suddenly, the phone didn't seem unreal, the deer did; the grouse, the ermine, the coyotes all seemed to have moved in on the territory staked out by the black wire and our cabin.

I looked around at our muddy yard, at the chips of birch, the axe, the maul, the sleds. We had carved a homesite in land that was once the range of the wild. Our deck crossed the old deer trail, we tore up a rabbit hutch to build the shed, and now the outhouse rose above the hazel brush where the vireo made her nest. We had connected our campsite to the chatty world around us. The intrusion was complete.

"The deer sure don't mind it, though," Jeanne said, watching the herd grow deer by deer for the dusk feeding. One by one they stepped across the wire and trotted to the corn. We had just begun to discover that the whitetail deer weren't bothered in the least by our arrival.

I gathered wood from the deck and built a fire in the woodstove. Jeanne poured water from the cans into a copper boiler; tonight was bath night, and preparations had to begin many hours in advance of the soaking. The room was soon filled with the aroma of woodsmoke, and we started to feel that we were alone again.

Jeanne scooped chili into bowls and we sat near the big window watching deer come and go as we ate. Dusk faded and our mirrored images grew brighter in the window, and the ritual of the bath began.

The woodstove was ticking hot. We took our turns stepping into a large shallow pan and dipped hot water from the boiler with a big sponge. We couldn't have imagined the exhilaration of a sponge bath in the days when we stood under a shower in the city. Here, once a week, using only three gallons of water each, a bath became an event. Watching the dirt and sweat of a hard week's work spill into the pan, feeling the heat of the stove and the massage of the sponge was relaxing and soothing to muscles not yet accustomed to axes, saws, and eighty-pound water containers. Into the pan below flowed the muddy waters of the week's work, and the world became a brighter place.

At last we donned our robes and sat close to the stove with a piece of warm apple pie. The cabin mouse darted from shadow to shadow, and as we doused the kerosene lamps and climbed into bed, the coyotes hailed the rising moon.

3

There was silence and peace in the morning air. The sun was still below the horizon and the silhouettes of birch against the dawn sky were filled with chickadees and evening grosbeaks waiting for the feeders to be filled.

Jeanne and I were buried in our warm quilt, building courage to leap to the floor and attend to our morning tasks. At the count of three we threw the quilt aside and slipped into warm robes. I checked the temperature: twenty-five degrees inside, ten degrees outside.

"There's ice on the water bucket," Jeanne said, using the handle of a knife to punch a hole through the thin sheet on our drinking water.

"We still have coals in the stove," I reported, putting pieces of birch bark into the small box heater. The bark ignited, and I laid aspen kindling on top of the coals.

While Jeanne went outside to attend to the bird feeders—a down vest over her robe and large boots on her feet—I built a roaring fire and put the coffee on the stove. Birds circled Jeanne's head as she carried the pail of seeds from feeder to feeder. There were no sounds but the peeping of happy birds and the crackling of the fire until I turned on our battery radio.

"...and drivers are cautioned to avoid the area on 35W southbound and the 46th Street exit," the announcer from the

Minneapolis radio station reported. "The accident has created a traffic back-up to 36th Street."

I remembered driving to work in the city. I could still feel a sigh and the tightening in my wrists as I held the steering wheel and prepared to park on the freeway until the mess had been cleaned up. There were appointments to keep, a plane to catch, and the city that hosted so much scheduled enterprise was forever throwing curves: accidents, slippery roads, construction, congestion. "The system doesn't work," I had said. But it did work in the long view, and for a minute I felt I missed the tension and excitement—just a little.

The deer almost beat Jeanne to their feeding station, and she smiled at me through the window, pointing to the large doe. It was Sleepy, the now nearly tame deer, who each morning let Jeanne come closer and closer before finally stepping back into the brush.

The radio continued to chatter about the aches and pains of getting to work on a Monday morning. Announcers summarized the troubles around the world and interviewed an expert on the economy. Jeanne came in and started breakfast. The temperature in the cabin had reached fifty degrees.

I felt a little guilty ducking out of the problems of the urban world, sitting in the woods by a warm fire of our own making while a hundred miles down the road thousands of people would be waiting for their buses. Dressing the kids for school, checking baggage at the airport, or waiting for an accident on the freeway to be cleared away seemed a harsh existence compared with our quiet life. We were warming our hands, watching deer and birds while the sun rose behind the trees. We were responsible only to ourselves this morning. There was no rear-view mirror to monitor, no horns, no brakes, no signs of warning to caution us against the perils of a workday morning. It was just Jeanne and me in the natural world, working to stay warm and fed and alert on a day that didn't need a name or a number or an allotment of hours. We thought about the contrast all the time.

The radio weatherman told the commuters that the drive home that night might be exciting in two to four inches of snow. The teletype racket in the background gave authority to his report and increased the excitement at the station.

"You'll keep an eye on it for us, won't you?" the announcer said.

"We sure will," the weatherman replied. "We're tracking the storm on radar, and we'll get back to you if there's any change."

Outside, the skies were blue with high cirrus and a cumulus build-up in the west. There was a spring snowstorm in the making, and we thought we'd better go out and gather firewood. A full woodbox is our savings account, and we learned early to make deposits before a storm.

Our woodlot is birch and aspen with a few oak and red maple scattered about above the dense understory of hazel brush, alder, and pin cherry. Because of the density, we had cut many trails to reach points of interest on our property. It was along these trails that we did most of our wood hunting. There was much standing deadwood, and the best of it was dry, barkless aspen, which burned fast to give us quick heat on a cold morning.

I laid a fire in the stove to keep the cabin warm, and then, taking saws and sleds, Jeanne and I set out on the trails. The outside temperature had risen to the mid-twenties, so we dressed lightly for our work. Sorel boots, corduroys, a cotton shirt, and wool sweater is plenty of clothing for working in the woods. We split up at a fork in the trail, hiked to our work sites, and filled our sleds rapidly.

During a moment's rest I could hear Jeanne's handsaw in the distance. The wind had picked up, and the evening grosbeaks, which often followed us back into the woods, were chattering in the tree tops. A chickadee was perched nearby, scolding me from a weathered stump that was once the base of a white pine. There were many such stumps on our property, and they told of the death and destruction that visited this place more than eighty years ago.

Before the white man arrived in these parts in the seventeenth century, this was the land of the white pine. They were tremendous trees, some of which grew more than a hundred feet tall and measured four feet across. As fur trading declined, the timber industry advanced rapidly, pushed by the need for lumber to build Midwestern cities. Skilled Yankee loggers from Maine and Vermont came into these woods shortly after the government bought the land from the Chippewa Indians in 1837. But, although the timber barons thought the pineries would last forever, the industry peaked in east- central Minnesota in the 1890s. The great pine had been taken and there remained in the forests only trees of lesser value: Norway pine, spruce, birch, and aspen. On the forest floors lay the slash—tinder-dry branches and tops of trees felled by the loggers.

By 1894 much of east-central Minnesota had been settled. Railroads had connected Minneapolis and St. Paul to the northern ports of Duluth and Superior. Lumber mills prospered, and towns were growing along the rail. This was no longer the frontier; homesteaders followed the lumber camps, and farmers burned the logged-over lands and planted hay and corn and potatoes.

A few flakes of snow were riding on the westerly winds; the sun was hidden behind the overriding bank of cloud. I could hear Jeanne's sled scratching along on the icy trail snow as she came to the ridge to meet me. For a moment I could hear the giant horse-drawn sleds of the loggers that worked this very land; their shouts echoed in this empty place.

There was drought the summer of 1894, and on Saturday, September 1st, brush fires were building in the hot, still air. Initially, there was little concern, the survivors said; fire was a tool, fire cleared the logged-over land. Smoke was always in the air those days. No problem.

But by midday the air was thick with smoke in east-central Minnesota, and the people of the growing towns watched nervously as the hot black clouds advanced from the south. Animals moved toward lakes and streams and swamps. Just west of what's now our property, men from a remote lumber camp loaded a buckboard with food and water and rifles. Then a wind came up from the southwest.

The survivors said that the winds pushed the brush fires, and a firestorm rushed the villages along the rail. In four hours, six towns were destroyed, and more than four-hundred people had died. They died in the lumber camps and they drowned in the creeks and rivers. Four-hundred square miles of forest were also gone. The lumber economy ceased to exist. Today, on the ridge, there are only charred stumps to remind us of a forest once quite different from our own.

Jeanne pulled her load up the trail. "Look what I found!" she yelled, holding up a curved piece of corroded metal.

The rusty metal strap had been part of a logging sled. Forged over the fires of a remote camp, it had been lost to the fire of 1894. Here, on this property, while the pine stumps smoldered, it lay red hot in the ashes of the sled. Here, as the aspen sprouted, the strap lay rusting in the decay of the logging camp. Then, as the trees grew to thirty feet and the hazel became a thick tangle and the bracken fern and aster covered the burnt ground, the strap was lost in time.

"I think the storm is here," Jeanne said as the dense bank of snow closed in around us. The flakes were large and wet and the clouds were dark as we pulled our sleds back down the trail to the cabin.

Inside, the soft wood heat quickly dried our sweaters, and we sat close to the big window with our coffee while the grosbeaks huddled in the feeder and snow collected on their backs. Several deer, moving single file down the trail, were coming to the corn that was now covered with snow. They pawed at the pile and ate quietly, occasionally looking around at a noise behind them in the woods. They were relaxed and only nibbled at the corn, for these were the snows of April and in a few weeks the southern winds would warm the ground and summer would be near.

"I can't wait until next winter," Jeanne said as we watched the snow. "We won't have this wilderness feeling for another six months."

It was true. By June the rumble of the tourists would be heard on the road. Cars and trucks and campers filled with tents and sleeping bags and children would pack into the state park. They would tour the country roads, and for a few months our world of quiet would be interrupted by the low din of traffic rushing, whining, scurrying through the weekends. The public would be at play in the woods.

I turned on the radio to see how the snowstorm was progressing in the city: "You're advised to use caution as you're homeward bound. The airport has reported two inches of wet snow, though the weather bureau reports clearing west of the cities."

The birds fluffed their feathers, the deer were watching something deep in the woods. Large tufts of wet snow fell from the trees.

"Dick! I see a bear—there on the ridge!" Jeanne cried.

I pulled the binoculars from their peg. "He's behind that big aspen—there!"

I looked, but as usual Jeanne spotted the animal before I did. It seemed pretty early in the year for a bear to be out and about. I reached for our field guide.

The first books on our bookshelves were field guides. They helped us through the maze of spring and fall warblers; through the mosses and lichens. We flipped the guide's pages while we counted lobes and poked at roots. At first, very little in the book looked like anything we saw. The sterile two- dimensional images of warblers never compared satisfactorily to the real thing darting about in the shadows of a dense bush. We chased flying things far into the woods, following with our books and binoculars while our quarry rested in the crotch of a tree twenty feet above our heads.

Eventually we got the hang of it by discovering habitats where we might expect to find warblers or crossbills or the first growth of wintercress. We began to see that nature wasn't random at all and that, like the inside of a great clock, our woodlot contained many different gears, each contributing something to the working of the whole. Our woodlot was a system. The comings and goings of wildlife, the growth and spread of bird's foot trefoil, all meant something that either reflected our presence or suggested a change for survival.

Bears, I read, might be expected to be about for a short time in April. I scanned the ridge again with the binoculars. No bear.

"Let's go out and have a look," Jeanne said. We got back into our boots—the radio was warning of slippery freeways—and stepped out into a winter wonderland.

The snow was very wet and we were glad for our Sorels, which are simply rubber shoes with heavy leather uppers lined with felt. They are very warm and comfortable as we work in deep snow or stand in mud while we're in low areas of the woods. We left deep, wet tracks as we hiked to the ridge.

As we gained the last hill, Jeanne spotted the tracks. The prints were large; the hindfoot was nearly eight inches long and four inches wide. Some of the size was due to the slushy nature of the snow, yet it was obvious we were on the trail of a respectable bear. Each of the five toes and claw marks were visible, and for a second I was chilled to think of a mammal of greater weight than Jeanne and I together, living on the woodlot with us. We decided to follow it.

The clear tracks crossed the ridge and stayed on the main trail to the bog. There, the bear waded through the dense, dry sedges and then moved out into the field of sphagnum moss, the bog.

The word "bog" comes from the language of the ancient Celtics and means something soft, something that gives or sinks. To our rural neighbors, the bog is a place to stay away from, and they call it "the swamp." About half our property is bog, and we learned early to walk it, to explore its mystery, to inhale its special fragrance. The bog gave us cranberries for Thanksgiving, a tree for

Christmas, and a look at insects, wildflowers, and birds that we wouldn't have seen on the high ground of the forest.

The bear led us to one of the many islands on the bog. There he had turned over a rotted birch log and slid down a bank back into the bog. I scanned the horizon again with my binoculars and saw nothing but leafless tamarack trees and black spruce.

He had to be in there—somewhere.

Bogs are the result of glacial action during the Pleistocene epoch that ended about ten-thousand years ago. As the glacial ice retreated, many small holes or kettles were created and these filled with water. Since there was neither inflow nor drainage, the vegetation accumulated and decayed, using up the oxygen in the water. Without oxygen, the partially decayed vegetation ceased to break down and peat was formed. Over time, the mat of vegetation thickened, and highly specialized plants found a home in the acid water. Thousands of years from now, the vegetable matter of our bog will compact and support meadowlands of common grasses and plants of the highlands.

As we walked among the hummocks of mosses, we felt as we had felt before—that we were in the land of the elves. In the distance we saw several deer bound from the spruce grove, jumping high over the mossy clumps as they headed for the distant shore. Our black bear was in the spruce.

"Let's go over to that island and see if we can spot him when he leaves the spruce," I said. "I want to see if he comes back to our side of the bog."

Jeanne nodded, her fists full of green mosses that she collected every time we were on the bog. "I hope there aren't any cubs around," she said, bending deep into a hummock and pulling out another long strand of moss. "We don't know whether it's a he or a she, you know."

Bears can be a problem. In the spring, when a female is out and about with her cubs, a meeting on the trail can be tense. We have always backed away from confrontations with bears whether it had cubs or not. Most of the time the bear beat us to the retreat.

When they come into our yard mid-summer, we stay inside and let them explore; when they come to the window, we do everything we can to scare them away. We have seen the work of a bear that broke into a cabin near us, and he didn't use the door. Most of the bear in our area weigh about two- or three-hundred pounds and have great strength for their size. When a bear is hungry, a wood frame building is no obstacle to its search for food.

On the island we found a log to rest on while I watched the spruce grove for a sign of the bear. The snowstorm was letting up and the sky to the west was clearing. We waited. A crow nearby gave our position away, and the deer, already nervous about the bear, stamped on the frozen ground and snorted. Jeanne was sorting her mosses and looking for pockets where they'd survive our walk home. Then the bear walked out of the trees.

I lifted my binoculars and watched him pick his way around a group of tamaracks and stop to sniff the breeze. He looked around as if he knew he was being followed. Although bears have terrible eyesight, their sense of smell is acute; the wind was in our favor, however, and it seemed to make him even more nervous. Thin from the long winter, the bear appeared to have too much skin for his gaunt frame as he moved toward our side of the bog; his coat shimmered in the muted light. Then he loped across the hummocks and gained the high ground. He stopped again and looked around. He was a beautiful sight posed against the white birch trees. He was a powerful form that made the whole of our land look fragile by comparison.

I didn't need binoculars now as we watched him rise on his rear legs and confidently rub his back against a large birch tree. His nose was in the air, his forelegs dangled at his sides, and the tree shook beneath his weight. He dropped to the ground and in a moment had disappeared into the woods.

"That was a good-sized bear," Jeanne said, catching her breath.

My heart was beating fast as we started back toward the cabin.

4

Spring was slow to mature. The sun climbed higher in the sky, the days grew longer and warmer, but the nights were very cold and the frost was still deep in the earth. There was little color in the transition; patches of rotting snow floated by day in the meandering streams of shimmering mud and were halted by a freeze at dusk. Yet there was excitement in the world beyond the cabin walls. The spring migrations had brought the woodcock back and juncos were everywhere, flocking around the feeders, squeaking their little conversations into the chorus of grosbeaks and chickadees. The spring peepers called from the marsh on warm days, and hawks circled above in the weak thermals of the rising sun. We felt serene in our life in the woods, we felt at peace, and for the first time in our lives, Jeanne and I relished every moment that we were awake. We were becoming a part of the world around us.

But the mail from our friends in the city was gloomy. There had been a divorce, an unsatisfactory job change, worries about money and general pessimism about the economy. There was uneasiness and a lack of confidence because Americans were still held hostage in Iran and the United States seemed unable to do anything about it. These were frustrating times for many, and one day we got a letter with a question: "Don't you two feel that you are running away from reality by living in the woods?"

Jeanne pushed the letter across the table. "I think she's saying that the world's on the brink of disaster and we aren't going to cocktail parties to groan about it," Jeanne said. I read the letter.

"She's right, you know," I said. "We should be down there beating our brains out to make mortgage payments and putting our money in the bond market. It's more than the American way of life to her—it's the only way to live. It's reality."

"Maybe we're doing our fair share by staying out of the way then," Jeanne said, watching a purple finch preen his feathers on the feeder. "But I can't feel guilty about living simply in a world that's eating itself up with complexity and hype for more and more and more."

Our coming to the woods had taught us early that we didn't need the extras that we had worked so hard to achieve in the city. We'd been to Europe, the Islands, the East Coast and West Coast. We'd tried to find pleasure in fine wines and new cars and airplanes and boats. But it wasn't until we walked this barren, boggy, brushy land that we had a shot of pure joy, and we came here to live to find out why.

We ate well, but less than we had eaten in the city. We didn't jog here; we worked long hours in the woods with purpose. We didn't relax in front of a television anymore; we were relaxed in our work.

Slowly we wound down to the pace of the natural world around us and began to sense a new reality. There were no seconds or minutes or hours here, and one day I threw my watch into a trunk under the bed. Soon the names of the days lost their meaning and we would go for weeks without using them. In the woods, time was an event. A marsh hawk's flight was not five minutes but a span that included low flight, a turn, a dive, and a reappearance over the bog. During the hawk's flight, a blue jay called, a deer appeared, and the sun was covered by a cumulus cloud. Events were not singular in our perception of them, but were overlapped, fused, and integrated with many other episodes, all of which had no beginning or end. It was time passing in the natural world. Of course, one might perceive the city as a stream of events, but to participate, one needs to select, focus, specialize. The production of goods and services requires it. There is purpose in developing a sense of the whole in nature. It is useful to understand every sound and feel the texture of mud on bare feet and the smell of rain. That is the reality of the woodlot. Our clock was the rising moon and sun, the shifting of constellations. Our calendar was the color change that made an ermine out of a weasel. Time was the crash one night when the cabin settled back on its foundation.

"What the hell was that?" I said, jumping up from my chair. A book on the shelf teetered and tumbled down onto the desk below.

"Must have been a sonic boom," Jeanne said. She peered out the window into the night.

We put our boots on and went outside. Silence. I pointed my flashlight to the trees that hung precariously over the cabin roof They were all there. Jeanne was looking toward the county road. "Maybe something blew up," she said. But there were no fires, no smoke. She walked around the cabin while I scanned the sky for signs of military jets on maneuvers.

"Dick, come here!" Jeanne yelled from the rear of the cabin. "It's back on the foundation." She flooded the northeast corner of the cabin with light. "Not a bad fit either."

Several weeks earlier, we had been startled to discover that a corner of the cabin was rising from the neat row of concrete blocks that formed its foundation. Day by day the crack grew larger, until the corner of the building was a full six inches off the blocks. We checked around with the local residents and gave them a good laugh.

"It'll come back down when the frost goes out," Ted said one night. "This here ground is so boggy, everything moves around in the spring. We got a window in the shed that won't open until December."

"Will it damage the cabin?" I asked.

"Ain't done nothing to it yet, has it?" he laughed.

41

It occurred to us that strange things had been happening all along. Pencils had suddenly started rolling off the desk. The front door would swing open on its own. A kerosene lamp was hanging with a list. One night we both looked up as the lamp began to swing, achieving another degree of tilt. "I think we're sinking," Jeanne said.

But no damage had been done. It just *looked* bad.

"Can you imagine how we'd feel if our hundred-thousand-dollar home in the city was coming off the foundation?" I said.

"We'd probably hire some hundred-thousand- dollar expert to come out and fix it," Jeanne said.

Control seemed to be a key to our new-found happiness. We felt in charge of our lives. There were no banks, government inspectors, or power and gas companies to dictate how we should live. We were left to our own devices to get up home and hearth as best we could. There would be no guarantee if we blew it; what we couldn't control, we lived with. That was, after all, what we had come to the woods to do: to live as closely as possible to the natural world, to live simply and to take care of ourselves.

When the cabin returned to its foundation, we made a note in the diary:

April 26. The cabin settled for the summer. Moon rise at 8:30. Temperature, 45 degrees. The evening breeze feels warm after weeks of damp cold. Wolves on the bog.

We walked out onto the moonlit bog to see if we could find the wolves. I wondered if the lessons learned here would change the way we lived if we ever moved back to the city. Probably, but we would soon begin to worry about the condition of our lawn. Our home would be our investment, and we would spend much time fussing over its upkeep. We would pay heavy taxes to improve the neighborhood and attend community meetings to protect our portfolio. Our time, our lives, would be spent crying out in defense of our property. That night, however, we were trespassing on the property of the wolf.

They are called coyotes by some, prairie wolves by a few, and brush wolves by the men who hate them. They are smaller in size than the gray wolf, or timber wolf. They are about the size of a strong German shepherd. They hunt alone or in pairs or, on rare occasions, in packs, and some say they mate for life. They are seldom killers of sheep, deer, and calves; they prefer mice, rabbits, and grouse in the deep winter snow.

It may be the howl, their song, that raises the hair on a man's neck. It may be the greenish-red shine of their eyes when a flashlight happens to catch one in its beam behind a shed at night. It is probably that they are seldom seen and always heard that has made them the enemy of most men. When they are seen, they are killed in these parts; and when a sheep is found dead, ripped at the throat, the pick-up trucks gather on the road and men with guns beat the brush and dig the dens of coyotes to take revenge.

We edged our way as quietly as possible along a growth of alder bordering the bog. The visibility was very good on the mossy field, and from the occasional yelp of a pup we knew they were out there. A cloud passed over the moon, and we were temporarily blind, standing in cold water to the ankles of our rubber boots. We made our move to the bog under the cover of dark, and I felt at once the sinking mat when we reached it. It was still warm from the day's sun; it was alive as all the woods and grasses are alive at night. The cloud drifted away from the face of the moon. We froze, watching.

There are stories about these shaggy wolves attacking a lonely farmstead on a winter's night, carrying off hens and murdering the sheep. It is possible, I suppose, that once in a great while, when the mice have burrowed and the hare are in short supply, the coyote will break into a farm. But a far greater danger to the husbandryman is the feral dog, the reject of a litter of domestic dogs. Rather than bear the expense of having these unwanted animals put down, people cart puppies off to the country and drop them along the road. If they survive the traffic, if they survive the cold, damp nights and the farmer's guns, if they learn to kill to eat, they may live to pack up with a band of their kind. They have no fear of man as the coyotes do, and they will raid his pantry and kill his calves, sheep, and hens. Not far from us, a farmer's wife was cornered by such a pack, and only her cries brought a gun to scatter the dogs.

We could not see the coyotes. We heard their murmurs: soft voices that rose with the mist from the hummocks of moss. We crouched low along the wet trail across the bog and were quiet. We were but shadows in the bright moonlight. A barred owl hooted and broke away from the black forest behind us, flying slowly across the bog and disappearing into the dark of the north. The coyotes talked in low voices as they moved slowly across our path several hundred feet away.

"Can you see them?" Jeanne whispered behind me.

"No, nothing. Can you hear them?"

I looked behind me and Jeanne was shaking her head, smiling at the excitement of being close to something wild, something free.

We didn't see the coyotes that night. Their voices faded and they were gone, dissolved into the night of new sounds and other creatures. A hare crossed our path as we returned to the cabin; a reckless hare will scamper in the presence of the owl and the wolf. And as we approached the cabin the deer were at the corn, silhouettes against the yellow oil light of lamps in the cabin window. They watched us a moment and melted, one at a time, into the woods.

Jeanne poured fresh water for tea, and I built a fire. The stove spread its warmth through the room. We turned the soft lamps low, and the moon filled the small space with its light. We felt, as we had felt many times before, that our living quarters were simply an extension of the world outside. Our walls were aspen boards that had once lived on this boggy place. Our fireplace stones had basked in the moonlight here for thousands of years before we had come. We were new, our smoke was new, and the thin glass between our heated room and the damp forest was all that set us apart.

Jeanne had spread large sheets of graph paper on the floor and was surrounded by brightly colored seed catalogs. The first warm breezes had stirred Jeanne's blood, and our garden was in the planning. From the window I could see in the moonlight the large brush pile that we had created while clearing a spot for the garden. Already a hare lived in the pile, and spring birds browsed the muddy clearing for seeds fallen during our cutting. We had pulled roots and followed the retreating frost deep into the clay earth, casting aside rocks and rotted stumps as we burrowed.

The plot was about twenty-five feet square, big enough, we thought, to grow vegetables for two. We were told by our neighbors that we could count on the deer to eat a quarter of our crops, that the raccoons might get away with another fourth, and that the squirrels and bear would split the rest. There was no practical fence tall enough to stop a jumping deer, no fence strong enough to stop a bear, and the weave had to be tight to keep the squirrels out. Jeanne was undaunted. "I'll worry about that when the time comes," she said, drawing long straight lines on her graph paper. Beans, tomatoes, carrots, beets, and potatoes fell into place on the plan. A few stalks of corn, sugar snap peas, and a variety of herbs filled out the paper garden. Then she added onions on the border and two long rows of strawberries.

"The deer will love it," I said when she had finished.

"You just wait," she said. "And watch—maybe you'll learn something."

Jeanne's philosophy of life had everything to do with the stomach. She saw in all of us simple foragers who would sooner eat than fight wars, walk in space, or merge large corporations. However complex our goals, Jeanne saw food at the bottom of them all, and I had to admit that a piece of warm apple pie could interfere with any of my projects anytime. The neighbors came for bread on cold winter days, and Jeanne mailed her spaghetti sauce all over the countryside at Christmas.

Once, when we were told that we should shoot blue jays because they would steal food from the chickadees and goldfinches, Jeanne simply developed a feeder that satisfied the jays and they soon left the smaller birds alone. We were also told to trap the red squirrels because they would tear the cabin apart to build nests. Jeanne gave them their own corn pile and access to a shed where they chewed and chattered and eventually built a nest. As a result of Jeanne's schemes to integrate wildlife by feeding them, we had days when blue jays, grosbeaks, chickadees, woodpeckers, nuthatches, red squirrels, gray squirrels, deer, rabbits, and raccoon were all eating together in the yard. A red-headed woodpecker drilled for seeds that Jeanne had jammed into the crotches of trees; a rough-legged hawk watched the noisy confusion below in apparent disbelief.

When the local folk came over for coffee they stared out the window in amazement. How was it possible for so many creatures to exist together peacefully? "Oh, they all have their own food," Jeanne would say, pulling a chocolate cake from the oven.

For days we worked the muddy garden, pulling roots, pushing large rocks aside, and spading the wet clay. I broke a shovel, bent the pitchfork, and when at last my gloves had no fingers and I ceased to walk erect like my near ancestors, Jeanne came running up the driveway from the mailbox with a package.

"The seeds came!" she shouted, running awkwardly in her large rubber boots. "They're here!" she panted, and we went into the cabin to see what had come.

One by one Jeanne laid the packages out for inspection and checked them off her list. Then, consulting her graph paper, she assigned the peas their plot and we went to work. All afternoon we prepared the surface for planting. The weather had been cool and dry for weeks. The soil was perfect, and we planted.

As we buried each seed the blue jays chatted in the trees overhead. A Franklin ground squirrel watched from a nearby rock. When we had finished the second row, the jays were in the garden.

"They just think we're feeding them," Jeanne said calmly as I watched the squadron of birds land on the first row. "I'll get them some corn."

Jeanne spread a row of corn along our plantings.

The jays watched. The squirrel watched. Then, as we continued to plant, we dropped a few corn kernels alongside each buried pea seed. The jays followed, gulping the corn. The squirrel just watched.

"I don't trust the squirrel," I said. "I think he knows something's up."

"We'll just keep our eyes on him, and I'll put a few sunflower seeds on his rock," Jeanne said.

Each morning we checked. The sunflower seeds were gone and the peas were still in the ground. "That's extortion," I said finally as I watched the squirrel wait patiently for his seeds. "Are you going to let that squirrel bully you like that? He knows damn well that there's pea seed under there, and the minute you stop paying him off we're through."

"I don't think so," Jeanne said. "I'm moving the sunflower seeds a little closer to the cabin from now on, and I think he'll forget about the garden."

It worked. Soon the squirrel was far from the garden. The blue jays figured they had already sacked the place, and except for an occasional deer, the animals stayed away from the crops. To this day I know that Franklin ground squirrel. He still smiles at me.

We managed to get the entire garden planted early in the season. The winds were warm and there was no rain. We opened the museum and summer was upon us. Each night we carried pails of water from the pond to the garden; it was drying rapidly. The talk in the area was the lack of moisture, but at first we didn't understand what they were really concerned about.

One afternoon, as we drove back to the cabin from the museum, we saw a giant column of smoke rising out of the east.

"That's a big fire going over there," I said. "It seems awfully dry to be burning."

As we got closer to the smoke we saw Department of Natural Resources trucks lined up along the road. Bulldozers and tank trucks were moving slowly across a field.

"That looks like a good-sized forest fire," Jeanne said. "If something like that got started near us, we'd cook before we could get down the road."

We were silent the rest of the way home. While Jeanne tended her garden I disappeared into the woods. I hadn't really looked at our home as fuel for a forest fire before. It had been leveled in 1894 and many years after that, but I hadn't thought about us facing fire. It didn't take me long to take stock of the dried brush along the ridge. I could see the smoke to the southeast. The fire would have to jump the St. Croix River and a blacktop road, but then there would be no stopping it. It would roar through our place in minutes. My mouth went dry.

How simple everything had been so far. Our stoves kept us warm in thirty-below-zero temperatures, the roof held off the snow and rain, we had no unwanted visitors. There was no danger because we were in control. We could guard against a fire of our making, but I hadn't thought about a blaze that might start twenty miles away. Suddenly I felt powerless. For the first time since our arrival I realized that something from the outside could get at us and we couldn't do a thing about it. I started back toward the cabin to help Jeanne water the garden. I could do that much at least.

5

Ted kicked at the dusty gray duff on the forest floor. The Pall Mall in his mouth was unlit. "You ought to brush out around your cabin," he said. "This stuff is too dry. If a fire gets going in here a fellow isn't going to be able to stop it."

"Brushing out" was something Jeanne and I had avoided. It meant clearing underbrush and thick stands of young trees. The idea was to create a large open space around buildings. It was fire protection and mosquito control, but it meant giving up bird nests at our window as well. We liked the look of the cabin sunk deep in a green thicket in summer. But as Ted and I walked in the still, dry air I could see the danger of living so close to the combustible brush.

The sun was orange in the hazy sky, a disc of light floating in the smoke of fires around us. For weeks much of southern Ontario had been burning. Fires in western Wisconsin and to the south had all contributed to the layer of smoke in the lower atmosphere. Tension was high, faces were grim, and we hauled extra water in buckets—just in case.

The days passed slowly. As we left our cabin to go to work at the museum, we hoped no one would throw a cigarette into the dry ditches and start a fire that would certainly end our new life in the woods. When we were in town the fire whistle would blow several times during the day. Volunteers rushed to the station, climbed aboard big yellow trucks, and headed out into the country. Hours later, tired and sooty, the citizen firefighters would return to tell of another hundred acres burned. We watched, we waited, and we soon learned to live with the threat of fire.

Nearly a month passed with no rain. Clouds would build and dissolve, the humidity rarely reached fifty percent, and one night, as we were going to bed, Jeanne saw a bright glow in the north. We went outside and climbed the ridge. The light grew brighter and flickered against the bases of the low clouds. All around us birds peeped and deer stamped and snorted. A rabbit startled us crashing through the brush nearby. The glow increased in brightness, then slowly died, and the north horizon dissolved into the night. The next day we visited the blackened acres. A lone deer stood in the ash that was once its feed.

Meteorologists reported sunny weather day after day. In the city, people enjoyed the warm, dry air after months of winter. Occasionally, at the end of a forecast, the weatherman advised travelers to the north country of forest-fire danger. "It's getting pretty dry up there, so be sure to put your smoking materials in a safe place, and remember that foresters advise no open fires."

In spite of the drought, woodland flowers bloomed and our garden began to show signs of life. We carried pails of water from the pond to water peas and beets, potatoes and tomatoes, and, one afternoon, Jeanne dumped several tadpoles into the carrots. We threw them back in the pail and went to the pond to have a look. Thousands of tadpoles, a great shadow on the pond floor, drifted from shore to shore. They appeared to be tadpoles of the green frog, and everywhere on the mudbanks of the shore were tracks of raccoon.

"Pretty hard to be worried about a fire that hasn't happened yet when life around here is as full as ever," I said.

Jeanne bent down to inspect the new fiddle heads of cinnamon fern. "If this fern was as worried about getting stepped on as I'm worried about someone starting a fire around here, I don't think it would have ever come out of the ground," she said. "I guess we're learning that there's more to life than worrying about what hasn't happened. We've got the best life we've ever had, here, in the middle of sixty acres of kindling, with our tadpoles and fern and—Dick, a deer!"

We were crouched low and when I finally saw her, the doe was at the far end of the pond. She looked at us, bobbing her head, and then stepped into the water to drink. Her coat was golden brown, and she twitched to shake off the deer flies. She drank in long slurps. The tadpoles, excited by the disturbance, moved quickly in a dark sheet along the bottom to the opposite shore. Blue jays, silent during their spring nesting, hopped from branch to branch on a tall aspen watching the three of us below.

"Do you think it's Sleepy?" I asked.

"No," Jeanne said, studying the deer carefully, "she's too small, but she isn't afraid of us. Look at the white patches above her hooves."

We watched the doe for some time. She would drink and raise her head. Looking around, she lifted her ears and twisted them like radar, picking up every little sound. A chipmunk was digging in the tall grasses nearby, and the doe moved her head from side to side to keep track of his progress. Rarely did she look at us.

"I think she's nursing a fawn," Jeanne whispered, studying the doe. "Look at her belly."

I was surprised that I hadn't seen it before, but I was getting used to being the last one to spot details in nature. The doe's belly was distended and appeared full. "Maybe she'll bring her fawn soon," I said a little louder than I should have. The doe's ears focused on me, and she wrinkled her brow. Jeanne gave me a dirty look. The chipmunk stopped digging and the blue jay flew silently into the forest. I sat back against the log and watched the clouds drift by.

The earth was warm and dry, the log was a perfect rest, and listening to the doe drink twenty feet from us was as relaxing as anything I could remember. I wondered why anyone could have worries when this peaceful scene was available for the price of a new car. I wondered how the hostages felt leaning blindfolded against an Iranian wall waiting for politicians to make decisions. I thought of the letter I had received a few days before from a guy I had worked with in the city. "I think you are vegetating out there," he wrote. "There is so much to be done, there's so much excitement here, and you pull up stakes and sit in the woods. You're not facing reality."

I read the letter again and again. The guy was right—to a point. Deep down, I knew that I was skipping out of a career, that I was not in the mainstream of events, but I couldn't agree that I was vegetating. Our life here wasn't monotonous. We had an ever-flowing stream of events to observe; we felt excitement such as we hadn't experienced before. We weren't merely living a physical existence. There was much creative thinking to be done to solve problems, and we were becoming well-read amateur naturalists. Nights were spent reading books that we had promised to read long ago. I found new joy in Treasure Island, Jamaica Inn, Madame Bovary, Jeanne had always wanted to take a vacation to read about Russia. Her nights were filled with the Tsarist collapse and the rise of the Bolsheviks. No, I thought, there had been less stimulation during our city life when we attended restaurant dinners and bland parties and spent long hours in front of a television.

But were we being passive? We were learning much. We were receiving all kinds of information, but what did we do with it? There was danger in that, a danger that was far greater than a forest fire. If we were living in a passive way, if we were receiving information but returning nothing, if we were becoming inert, our experience would amount to nothing. In our work at the museum, we researched, designed, and built exhibits, gave lectures and tours. There was action there, but the greater part of our existence was clearly maintenance of our life at the cabin. I had been a writer in the city and I had expected to write from the bog. I hadn't. It was time to respond. As the clouds thickened overhead, I began a story in my head, a story of a deer that came to a pond to drink.

"Thunder," Jeanne said quietly.

I looked up, and the deer stepped quickly into the woods. I looked again at the clouds I'd been watching. They were full, round, and fat cumuli, building rapidly. "We might get some rain this time," I said.

Jeanne was laughing. "I think I can taste it already," she said, getting up. "Let's go up to the ridge and have a look."

We dashed along the dry trails and gained the ridge in record time. Far to the southwest, great black clouds welled up and boiled, moving toward us. Lightning flashed from cloud to cloud and from the clouds to the ground, dancing like sequins on a deep blue velvet dress. Thunder crashed, and from where we stood it appeared that the long shafts of rain were dragging across the ground from the great cumulonimbus cloud. The light winds that had been dry and dusty for a month were now stronger, cool, and damp. Birds were giddy with song as large raindrops splashed in the chalky duff and rolled among the dried leaves like BBs. A drop rolled down Jeanne's cheek—I thought it was a tear—then another and another. We laughed and walked home slowly, getting wet, cool and happier with each step.

Two inches of rain fell in three days. Much of it ran off the high ground and filled the pond, ditches, and creeks; but as the early days of June passed, more clouds formed and more rain fell. The fire danger was over, and city weathermen sadly reported, "You aren't going to get a tan today."

I could easily remember long, hot summers in the city when the beaches were the center of my world. Fair weather was good weather; rain was bad. Thunderstorms were distant and troublesome events, something violent in the sky high above the tall concrete and steel buildings. The city defended itself against the rains with elaborate storm sewers, pedestrian shelters, and shiny aluminum rain gutters. Here, on the woodlot, the rainstorm was as necessary as a heartbeat. The storm was loud and close and part of the boggy soil that vibrated with every clap of thunder. Here, the trees swayed in strong wind and recoiled from the shock of a lightning strike. Here, the rain was life itself, as much a part of the rhythm of continuance as the sun, the wind, and the snow.

The green haze of leaves in the treetops had become full-bodied, and the forest closed in around the cabin. Brightly colored warblers sang in the underbrush, and a cedar waxwing moved quietly among the alder growth on the shore of the bog. Everywhere we hiked we packed binoculars, field guides, and notebooks. As we learned more about our land we became involved in the day-by-day struggle for life of plants and animals. We were especially concerned about the ovenbird. Her nest, an oven-shaped domed collection of grasses and leaves, was located on the ground just off the trail to the ridge. We had seen the bird walking along the trail, and one day we spotted her sitting in the nest. We paid little attention so we wouldn't disturb her. She was a warbler, olive-backed, with a striped breast. She had five eggs.

"How can she expect to survive right here on the trail?" Jeanne asked one day after we had passed the nest site. "Look, raccoon tracks all over the place. They love birds' eggs."

We watched the ovenbird's nest for several days. Then, as we walked by late one afternoon, the nest was in shambles.

"Somebody really tore it apart," I said. "Look, here's a part of the roof." I held the fragile mat of grass and leaves in my hand, amazed at the incredible diversity of plants that the warbler had gathered.

"And here's a piece of shell," Jeanne said sadly. "I wonder if the birds had hatched."

We saw no more of the little ovenbird, nor heard her tea-cher song at dusk, but we did see raccoons. Every evening a pair swaggered into the clearing beyond our window and settled down in the corn pile. Pushing each other with their ample rumps, they chewed, open-mouthed, loudly into the night. When the deer came, the raccoons grudgingly moved aside and shared the pile. The deer, hesitant at first, soon pushed their way in and chewed as loudly as their corn mates. Inside the cabin, with the windows open, we could hear the constant crunch, crunch throughout the evening. Occasionally a raccoon growl, or the stomp of a deer hoof, warned of a territory problem, but soon the chewing resumed its steady pace.

One night when the chewing stopped, Jeanne and I looked up from our books and listened. There was no sound. In a moment we heard the brush cracking and then silence again. We peered out of the window into the night, but saw nothing. I reached for my flashlight, and we went out onto the deck. When I focused the light, Jeanne was ecstatic. "A skunk," she said. "I knew we had to have them! And I have a name already picked out: Daisy." The skunk squinted into the flashlight beam, and I turned it off.

Several nights later things around the corn pile had returned to normal. The skunk hadn't returned. One morning just before the sun rose, Jeanne came running back from the outhouse, white as a sheet. "I saw her! She was alongside the outhouse, and when I opened the door she was right there!" "Who?" I asked.

"Daisy! She had her tail up and everything." "Well, you probably surprised her," I said, trying to focus my eyes on the outhouse in the faint dawn light.

"She surprised me" Jeanne said. "Every morning I go up the hill on the same path, open the door...well, she scared me."

We walked up the trail—making as much noise as possible— and when we peered around the corner of the outhouse she was there to meet us, rear-end first. She did a little dance with her back feet, and the next thing we knew we were back on the cabin deck, gasping for breath.

"Did you see her do that with her feet?" I asked, panting.

"Yes. I think that means they're ready to squirt you."

"Are we going to let one little skunk keep us away from the john?" I said with certain determination.

"*I* am," Jeanne said. "And she isn't little." Jeanne walked off into the woods.

Daisy was gone by sunrise, but late in the afternoon, while the deer were in the yard, she returned. The deer had been watching the trail for some time, and we were curious about what had been attracting their attention. As we watched, Daisy appeared at the entrance of the trail and the deer froze. They watched her, bobbing their heads. When she was satisfied that there was no danger in the yard, she started toward them. The deer stumbled over each other to get out of the way. One leaped gracefully over a fallen log and another slipped before she bashed off into the brush. Daisy continued for a few feet, then stopped. She looked behind her and then continued her shuffle toward the corn. Several feet behind her trailed four little skunks in single file. I knew Jeanne was straining her reservoir of names.

"What are you going to call them?" I asked, smiling.

"One, Two, Three, and Four," she said, watching the little visitors with her binoculars. I didn't ask how she was going to tell them apart.

The skunks poked around the corn for a few minutes, and then, invisible to us, Daisy organized her little band and they marched across the yard, around our deck, and up the trail toward the outhouse. Four small tails and one large one swished and swayed deliberately as they climbed the rise.

"I suppose the outhouse is going to be their home," Jeanne said sadly.

"Most likely a hunting ground," I said, flipping pages of the field guide. "I think they've found mice or something up there."

Later, after the moon had risen, I went to the outhouse. I'd forgotten about the skunks and didn't think about them until I was comfortably seated. The door was wide open, and the moonshine on the birch trees had captured my attention. There was a crack of a twig—and just that fast I remembered the skunks. I pulled the door shut and waited. I listened. I held my breath and listened. An owl hooted far off on the bog, spring peepers were in chorus at the pond. My imagination clearly pictured five skunks just outside the door. Something brushed against the back wall of the outhouse. My heart now thumped as loud as any of the night sounds. I sniffed.

The field guide said I might be able to smell the skunk before I saw it.

I listened, then opened the door a crack. In the moonlight everything on the ground looked like a skunk—a piece of birch bark, dead leaves, a stick. I opened the door wider and saw the cabin lights down the path. Without thinking, I jumped out of the outhouse and trotted down the trail pulling up my pants as I ran. If I was going to get sprayed, it was going to be on the run. Nothing happened.

On the deck I gathered my wits, buckled my belt, and entered the cabin cool and calm but with a fair pulse rate.

"See anything?" Jeanne asked absently, as we always did when one or the other had been abroad on the land.

"No," I panted, "but the moonlight is fantastic on the birch."

The next morning, Jeanne asked why I had left the outhouse door open.

For several nights, the doe we had seen at the pond seemed nervous in the yard. She browsed some and spent long stretches looking back into the brush. We scanned the forest's edge with binoculars looking for trouble, but found none. Then, late one afternoon, she came to the clearing and stood facing the cabin. Her usually serene face looked tight and worried. After a few moments spent sniffing the wind, she walked slowly toward the cabin and stopped. Suddenly, a fawn appeared at the edge of the yard. It walked on shaky legs to the corn and was followed by another, smaller fawn. The doe looked at us standing in the window and bobbed her head.

Jeanne was beside herself with excitement. "She's brought them to show us," she said.

"Maybe she just brought them to the corn," I replied, sorry that I didn't share Jeanne's bright outlook on the relationship between man and animals.

But they were the loveliest creatures I had yet seen on the place. They were cute beyond description as they tested the favorite haunt of the older deer. Their legs were so wobbly that each step's outcome was always in doubt. Their ears flicked back and forth as they watched a squirrel scurry about the edge of the corn. They lowered their heads to sniff the squirrel, and they fell back as it ran beneath their legs. Everything on the woodlot was new and exciting to them: a blue jay's flight, the wind in the trees, a rabbit in the brush, Jeanne and I standing in the light of the kerosene lamps. As we settled down to our books that night, we watched the three deer move about the yard under a bright moon. At last, because the coyotes were getting close, the doe herded her fawns off into the night, deep into the birch.

One morning we awoke to a loud rattling *k-r-r-o-o, k-r-r-o-o*. We jumped out of bed and ran to the window. Again the prehistoric sound echoed in the still air. We dressed and went out for a look. The sound seemed to travel across the bog and to the west. Moments later it would return. *K-r-r-o-o, k-r-r-o-o*. We stepped out into the fog and worked our way to the bog following the mournful wail.

Then, through the mist, we saw the shadow of a giant bird. Flying nearby was another. Together, they flew like two giant crosses, and the sound of their wings thumped and hissed as they passed overhead.

Their voices again shattered the stillness, and we hiked back to the cabin eager to find out what sort of creature had moved into the bog. According to the field guides, we were looking at sandhill cranes. We gulped down our breakfast and went out to have another look; this time we took binoculars and the guide. We stayed on the main trail that led to the large bog at the rear of our property. We had an idea that the birds might be nesting there.

The woodlot had changed dramatically in those last weeks of June. The drought had slowed the early growth, but the late rains had given the low woodland a lusty spring smell. The growth of the ferns had covered our trail, and we wasted time retracing our path. "Let's cross over here and get out on the bog," I said. "We're going to end up going around in circles in this jungle."

Finally we made it to the bog and started toward an island where I thought we could get a good view.

"What's that?" Jeanne said, pointing to an object that appeared to be standing on the shore of the island.

I looked at the thing with my binoculars, but I was looking into the sun and the image made no sense. Whatever it was, it didn't move; it looked like a branch of a dead tree. "I don't remember seeing it before," Jeanne said.

As we approached the island the thing opened huge wings and pushed off, flying low and away from us across the bog.

"The crane!" I shouted, but Jeanne was already watching the bird as it turned.

"They must be nesting around here. Let's leave them alone," Jeanne said. We turned back.

We were silent as we walked. It was hard to talk while hiking the bog, struggling to get a sure foothold and climbing over the hummocks of moss. But we were also sharing the same thought: We had picked a place to live that was out of the mainstream of exotic places, yet we were surrounded by an incredible diversity of life; a fragile web of wild existence that hadn't been disturbed by man in search of wealth or recreation. We were both wondering how long it would stay that way.

6

On June 21st we had breakfast with the sun in our eyes and fresh strawberries from the garden. The sun was by that time positioned directly over the Tropic of Cancer, giving us—and the strawberries —nearly sixteen hours of daylight.

Since our arrival in March, we had crammed as many chores as possible into few hours of daylight and spent long hours of darkness tending kerosene lamps and waiting for daybreak. Now, with sunrise at five in the morning and sunset at nine, we spent our time like the new rich, squandering our hours of warm wealth wandering about the bog and woodland, looking in on the affairs of the wilderness around us. Never so conscious of daylight when we lived as parasites on the system of electricity and oil heat, we were now developing a sense of our world as an orbiting planet subject to seasonal variation. We were coming to understand the simple physical laws that we had presumably learned in grade school. Knowing something and understanding something are two very different aspects of education. We were, at middle age, coming to an understanding of the natural world.

There were times when we sensed rain in the air, and with no further speculation each of us quietly moved firewood into the shed. Dry firewood cooked our meals and boiled our water; damp firewood smoked. When the birch swayed in a summer wind we gathered the dead branches for kindling. Birch bark, the best firestarter we know, loosened and fell and blew about the woodlot until Jeanne and I found it and carried it in our pockets with every intention of storing it in the woodbox. Often, however, it stayed in our pockets. Once, while I was talking earnestly to a group of visitors in the museum, I managed to grab a handful of bark instead of my handkerchief to intercept a sneeze. The visitors were not impressed, and we worked at leaving our woodsy habits at home. Jeanne was the one who was forever picking up kindling while we were in town. I would often see her talking to a clutch of women and absent-mindedly pick up twigs in the street and jam them into the pocket of her corduroy blazer.

We also developed a dislike of indoor plumbing. After several months of outhousing, flush toilets seemed primitive and unclean. Bacteria breaks down waste material very efficiently in the woods, and the thought of wastes traveling through miles of sewer pipe to a processing plant became an unpleasant idea. We began to understand why rats favored cities and dense human populations.

We were beginning to understand that the greatest difference between us and our city cousins was attitude. We *had* to accept the phenomenon of the natural world; it was part of our every waking minute. In the city, strong fortresses had been developed to defend against everything that nature had to offer. We became conscious of how silly umbrellas appeared, how senseless tanning creams and useless bug lotions were. We knew why people used products to keep dry, tan, and itchless, but we couldn't agree on the technique. To us rain, sun, and bugs were part of each day. We routinely got wet, burned, and bitten.

Several days after the solstice, we had a call from a city friend who proposed a visit to our cabin. He and his wife planned to pack a tent and drop in on us for a day or two and see what it was like to live in the woods. When they arrived they were disturbed that they couldn't drive their car up to the cabin door. A few moments later we saw why: The tent they planned to spend the night in was at least a twelve-man affair. They had packed cots, coolers, and a battery-operated radio-television-stereo machine that came with a collapsible metal stand. She had brought a suitcase full of lotions and potions to protect her from mosquitoes, flies, harmful sun rays, dry skin, and poison ivy. He had brought an equally large suitcase full of cameras and lenses, with an "outdoor" rainproof pouch to protect the expensive equipment.

We found a nice place for our friends to erect their canvas building and helped them fill the place with their necessities. Jeanne and I were at first concerned that we had misunderstood their intentions and had the fleeting thought that they might stay a week. Indeed, they had brought with them food enough for a month.

They came into the cabin when their subdivision was complete and poured gin and tonics all around. We gossiped while they looked around at our wooden room and swatted at flies and mosquitoes. "They carry diseases," Babe said, dressed in fashionable khakis. "You can't be too careful."

"Hey, I'll get our spray from the tent," Fred said. "That does wonders."

"Why don't we go for a hike instead," Jeanne suggested. "I'll bet when we get back the flies will be gone."

"That'd be great," Fred said, stretching. "There's nothing like a walk in the woods to build up an appetite. We'll get our things."

Fred and Babe went to their tent. When the door had closed behind them, Jeanne shook her head. "What happened to them?" she said. "They used to be kind of mellow people."

"Maybe *we've* changed," I said.

Fred and Babe returned dressed in L.L. Bean bush jackets. They were loaded with cameras and lenses, and Fred's hiking boots were suitable for a trek in the Himalayas. Babe sprayed herself with insect repellent and toted a day pack of cigarettes, wine, and cheeses. Fred was taking pictures before we left the yard.

"Like to get one of you two in the trees there," he said, fiddling with lenses and an automatic motor drive. The machine whirled through several frames, and he was satisfied. Babe sprayed her wrists with bug spray, and we were off.

Sometime later, after much loud talk and the clatter of cameras and cans in the day pack, Fred told me that he was surprised not to see many animals. Babe had cornered Jeanne and was explaining the pleasures of shopping at an outfitter's. "You know, you and Dick ought to come down to the city and go to the place with us. They have the neatest back packs. I got this one there and it goes with my jacket perfectly." From time to time Jeanne caught my eye and gave me the signal to speed up the jaunt. We had gone only a quarter of a mile, yet our friends were showing signs of boredom. "I'll tell you, Dick, we went out to Montana for a trail ride last year, and we saw animals that would drive you and Jeanne crazy. God, they were all over the place."

"And remember the cook-out?" Babe said. "They had steaks for everyone this thick." She showed us with her fingers and then slapped at her face. "And they didn't have any bugs out there."

Jeanne produced a growth of lichen that she had spotted on a snag of dead aspen and began to talk about it.

"Don't *touch* it! Oh, you shouldn't touch it,"Babe exclaimed, holding her cigarette away from her face. "You never know what's poisonous."

"This isn't poisonous," Jeanne said in a low voice. She broke off a piece to show them.

"Oh, ick," Babe said.

"Hey, why don't we get a fire going and have a little lunch," Fred said. "I'll get some wood, and we'll toast some of those English sausages we brought. They make the day for me on a hike."

"It's too dry to have fires out here," I said. "Why don't we just go sit on that log and have a little wine, if you like."

While they busied themselves in the day pack, I looked at Jeanne and sighed. Fred and Babe were not interested in rough woodland; they didn't have the slightest curiosity about anything around them. Jeanne edged closer to me.

"The deer are here," she whispered. "Do you think we ought to tell your friends?"

"They're our friends," I said. "Might as well. It would give them something to talk about anyway." I looked up and saw the three does not more than twenty feet away, almost hidden in the brush. Fred was trying to get a new corkscrew to work while Babe brushed bits of leaf and grass off her pants.

"Listen," I said calmly, "there are three deer standing just over there in the bushes." That was all I had to say. Fred dropped the bottle and corkscrew and fell flat on his stomach grabbing his camera case. "Okay, everyone quiet!" he hissed while he fitted one of the cameras with an enormous lens. Babe froze and turned her head in small arcs looking for the deer. "Where are they?" she whispered.

"Just over there, in the bush....."

"Shhh!" Fred said, fitting the motor drive onto his camera. The thing went off, *zip-zip-zip-zip,* while he was fooling with it. "Damn!" he said. And then Babe caught sight of the does, who seemed to be enjoying the confusion.

"There they are, Fred!" she whispered. She lay down at her husband's side and directed his eyes to the bush where she had seen the animals. *Zip-zip-zip,* the camera whirred as the deer watched and Jeanne and I sat on the log drinking wine.

"They're gone, Fred," Babe said, standing to brush the leaves from her outfit. "Did you get a good one?"

"I don't know, I couldn't get the motor drive in place fast enough, and you couldn't really see them very well. I wonder what they were doing here?"

"They *live* here," Jeanne said.

His wife looked around. "I feel watched," she said. "What other little surprises do you two have for us out here?"

"Well, there's a b—"

"*Beaver,*" I interrupted. "There's beaver all over the place."

An hour later we returned to the cabin and our friends retired to their tent. On the return hike, Fred had lectured me on nature photography while Babe dragged far behind with Jeanne, favoring a twisted ankle that she'd suffered in a remarkable fall over a log.

"They'll be gone tomorrow morning," I said to Jeanne while we fired the woodstove. "I wouldn't have believed that they would act like this. They've been hikers for years."

"On polished trails, with guides and marked campsites," Jeanne said. "They aren't comfortable in the brush."

Supper with our friends was a lengthy affair with much wine and talk of Fred's adventures in far-off places. Babe questioned us at length about choosing the bog and the ratty woodland for a homesite instead of the scenic mountains and streams of the West.

"You two should see it again, really. There are beautiful sites for sale now on the mountain sides, even condominiums."

"Dick," Fred said, "picture waking with the sun in your eyes and looking out the window over miles of tall pine and spruce forests. Fantastic lakes, skiing right out the back door, animals. I've seen a lot of North America, but I've never seen more wildlife than in the mountains."

"What kind of birds have you seen?" Jeanne asked. "Birds?" Fred reached over and held Jeanne's wrist. "Kid, when there are antelope and bighorn sheep and bear living with you on the same mountain, you stop worrying about birds."

"We *like* birds," Jeanne said.

"I saw an eagle at Jim's condo—remember, Fred?" Babe poked at a mushroom in her salad and moved it over to the side of the plate.

"Oh, yeah, if you like birds I suppose they're out there," Fred said. "Hell, everything's out there. One day we packed a busload of people— remember, Babe—and went over to the valley and photographed a deer herd. Jesus, they were beautiful, not over a hundred yards from the bus." "The deer are here," Jeanne said suddenly, looking out the window. Eight does and their fawns were coming into the yard for the corn piles and clover.

"How'd you get them to do that?" Fred said, sliding off his chair and tiptoeing over to the big window. He crouched behind the sofa and peered out at the herd, which was peering back at him. "Hold it, Fred," he said to himself. "You don't want to spook them. Look, Babe."

Babe was looking. Salad was falling into her lap from her uplifted fork. Her mouth was wide open.

"Dick, there must be a dozen of them!" Fred said. "You know what you ought to do," he began, but he stopped as Jeanne left the cabin. He watched her cross in front of the big window, fill a coffee can with corn, and walk toward the herd. The deer stepped back into the bush, but returned to the corn when Jeanne headed toward the cabin. Fred got up off the floor, and Babe brushed the salad off her khakis into a napkin. Jeanne came in and set the coffee can by the door.

"Do they always come into your yard?" Babe said. "Every night, unless the bear is here," Jeanne said. I looked at her and shook my head.

"Bear?" Fred said.

"There aren't bear here, are there, Fred?" Babe asked.

Jeanne found our snapshots of a black bear that occasionally came by to ransack the bird feeders.

Fred said, "You ought to get the wardens over here to get rid of that fellow. He can be dangerous."

"Do you get rid of bears in the mountains?" Jeanne asked, clearing the table.

"Oh, no, that's their home. Your bear is a rogue."

"Why do you think he's a rogue, Fred?" I asked. "Well, it stands to reason. Bears are at home in the wilderness, not here, a hundred miles from the cities and a couple miles from a farm."

Jeanne poured coffee. "Yet you have wild bears a couple of miles from your mountain-top condo,"she said.

"Oh, no," Babe said. "They're in the parks where they belong."

Fred said, "Well, I'd be cautious, Dick. Bears can't be trusted."

"We don't trust our bears," I said.

"You have more than one?" Babe said.

Fred and Babe settled down and watched the deer move silently through the yard. The fawns played while the does tried to keep some order. Once in a while a youngster, too frisky for his mother's sensibilities, was whacked on the head by the doe's sharp hooves. There was little talk now as the four of us sat in the darkening room. Soon we were watching mere shadows move about in the tall birch. Jeanne got up from the table and lit a kerosene lamp. A warm glow filled the wooden room.

"It's very comfortable in here," Babe said. "It's so quiet. I can't believe how quiet."

Fred was lying back against the couch still dangling his camera. Film bulged in the pocket of his nylon jacket.

"I'd better get him to the tent," Babe said. "We've got a lot of unpacking to do to get ready for bed." "Babe, why don't you and Fred stay in the cabin tonight," I said. "Jeanne and I will go out to the tent. You just relax."

Babe protested, but we insisted, and after showing her how to douse the light, Jeanne and I went up the trail to the tent. We had often camped along the trail when we had been weekenders, and the sound of unzipping the tent door brought back a flood of memories. We settled in on the cots and lay awake under the stars and listened to the coyote concert.

"I wonder what they think of coyotes," Jeanne said.

"I think they're asleep," I said. "Remember how much of the wildlife we missed when we came up here on a Friday night? I fell asleep as soon as we unpacked the car."

"Do you ever miss those days?" Jeanne said softly in the dark.

"I was just thinking about that. There was something secure about living in both worlds, about having a job that really meant something and thinking about going to the cabin on Friday afternoons."

"You used to load the car and pick me up at the bank."

"And we talked all the way up here about the day that we could break away and live here full-time. There was never any doubt in our minds that we would do it."

"I wonder if Fred and Babe will do it. They say they will someday."

"I don't think so. I think when they've spent a week on one of their jaunts they're pretty happy to get back to the city. They have a heavy social life, and I'd bet they couldn't stay away from a party long enough to let the woods get into their blood."

Jeanne was silent for a moment and then she said, "That sure isn't what happened to us. Remember that February hike we took when we sat on a log trying to decide whether to go back for the office party? We thought this was more important."

"A freezing cold night, and I couldn't get a fire started."

"Yeah, we just lay there in our sleeping bags like this and talked about living here someday. Seems like a long time ago."

The morning sun woke us early, and we tiptoed back to the cabin to make coffee. Fred and Babe were fast asleep. I loaded the cans into the car and went to Ted and Louise's for water. When I returned, Jeanne was sitting on the deck drinking coffee.

"Aren't they up yet?" I asked, dragging a heavy milkcan of water up from the car.

"Haven't even stirred," Jeanne said. "Maybe they're dead."

"Why don't we go get some wood before the mosquitoes wake up," I said. "Then we can get up a big breakfast and find out what they're going to do for the rest of the day."

In less than an hour we returned with a wheelbarrow full of dry aspen and birch. We had just finished stacking it on the deck when the door opened and Fred looked out at us, squinting into the sun.

"I was wondering when you guys were going to get up," he said. "I thought you country folks were up and at 'em before the sun."

"We were," Jeanne said. "I made some coff—"

"Babe found coals in the stove and brewed up some coffee for you sleepy heads. I was just going to bring it out to the tent."

"There was coffee."

"Naw, we made some fresh. No use drinking last night's. Hey, what a gorgeous day! Any deer out there last night?"

Jeanne looked at me. I looked at her, and we went inside to start breakfast. The room was smoky.

"How do you get this dumb thing to stop smoking?" Babe said, fanning with a newspaper. Jeanne opened the draft.

"You sleep pretty well?" I asked Fred, who was tying his heavy-duty hiking boots.

"Never slept better," he said. "I never want to hear that you two are roughing it up here. God, that bed's like a cloud. Where'd you get it?"

"We made it," I said.

"Fred, they should make one for us," Babe said, holding the broken egg shells Jeanne was handing her.

We ate breakfast and chatted about friends back in the city. Once or twice I looked up at Jeanne and she smiled, shrugging her shoulders. Nothing had changed. The same people were skiing in the same places. They had all vacationed in St. Thomas, and those with children were worrying about schools and drugs. Everybody was concerned about investments.

"I'm buying a little gold now and then," Fred said. "Not much, but just a piece here and there to keep in the safe. The economy is going to improve, I'm sure of it, but it doesn't hurt to have a few bucks liquid, you know."

"I suppose you two are buying gold, too," Babe said. "Everyone's doing it."

"Our gold is out there," I said, pointing out the window at the birch. "That's our heat and our cooking fuel no matter what the value of the dollar. Jeanne's garden is our gold, too. Looks like we're going to have enough tomatoes to hold us for the winter."

"That's cute," Babe said.

"I suppose you have guns to fight off the vandals from the city, eh?" Fred said. "When the great crash comes, you're ready. Actually, you guys ought to face reality. It doesn't hurt to come out here and play woodsmen for a while, but someday you're going to want to come back."

"We don't have any guns, Fred," I replied. "We don't think there's going to be a crash. We're just trying to get along doing for ourselves and enjoying the woods while we still have woods to enjoy. We aren't hurting anyone out here."

Our friends spent the day potting about their tent and helping us with chores. Babe worked with Jeanne, carrying water to the garden from the pond. Fred and I split wood and later hiked out onto the bog so he could take pictures. When his tripod started to sink into the sphagnum moss, he gave up and we hiked.

"There's a nice feel about this place, Dick," he said when we had gained high ground. "I don't know what it is, but there's a feeling of loneliness here that I haven't even sensed in the mountains." "I think that's part of what attracted us to the bog," I said. "It's wasteland to most people."

Fred and Babe had relaxed. They were cheerful, they were the friends that we remembered— but they were also going to cut short their visit. After dinner they packed their bags, broke camp, and after a flurry of goodbyes departed.

Several weeks later we received a small package of slides that Fred had made of the deer, the cabin, and Jeanne and me. We held them up to the sky.

"They're not very good," Jeanne said.

"Fred had fun doing it," I said.

"Do you think we'll ever see them here again?"

"I don't think so. We don't live in a very exotic place. Most of the outdoor people we know prefer lakes and streams and mountains and a lodge with a stone fireplace. We live alone on a misty bog—which is why we came here, isn't it?"

7

In the photograph that Fred had taken of Jeanne and me standing proudly in front of the cabin, all appeared serene; you couldn't see the mosquitoes. But you didn't have to listen very carefully to hear them, and you certainly would have felt them. The spring drought had only slowed their birth rate; by the end of June, what the creatures had lost in time, they'd made up in numbers and ferocity. When we went outside, the feeding frenzy began. There was no repellent that gave us any protection, so we slapped them, we wore netted hats, we built smudge fires, and then we took a lesson from the deer—we ran.

We ran to the outhouse; we ran to the mailbox, to the garden, to the woodpile. We stepped out on the deck at sunrise, stretched, said good morning to Mother Nature, and then we ran.

Mosquitoes ruined the pleasure of our outdoor baths. Mosquitoes made sleep impossible. Mosquitoes turned up at lunch in our sandwiches. They were in our soup, in my shaving cream, and there was always one floating in the Kool-Aid. We picked at them, we slapped at them, we itched and scratched. Finally, too tired to resist any longer, we let them eat us alive.

The deer were having their summer troubles, too. We watched them leap into the yard bucking and twitching with wild eyes as they tried to shed deer flies. The female deer fly sucks blood, and though she's only a little larger than the common house fly she's a lot meaner. When we were hiking and happened to cross a trail used by the deer, there would always be a couple of deer flies to escort us through the territory. They would buzz around our heads —around and around. Swatting at them served no useful purpose; again we ran.

The deer spent the better part of the deer-fly season running through dense hazel, which brushed the insects from their bodies. They browsed long hours far out on the bog where the faint breezes of July soothed them and where the infrequent rainstorms could take effect.

The days were very hot and damp, and Jeanne and I increased our bath schedule as water supplies permitted. We were hauling water cans twice a week now and dreaming of showers and bathtubs and cool swimming pools loaded with chlorine. The summer woods were cool at the beginning of July, but soon the heat worked its way deep into the brush where there was no wind to stir the humid air. While insects flourished, mammals were sullen and quick-tempered, and Jeanne and I brooded indoors, planning improvements for the place. Our own well topped the list of such projects.

Getting water in our part of the country was a problem. Most of our neighbors had drilled wells two- or three-hundred feet deep and often pulled an iron-tasting liquid from the bedrock. At fifteen dollars a foot, a drilled well was a sizable investment and something we couldn't afford. The alternative was a shallow well, but folks worried about contamination from the bogs. What concerned them was tannin, or tannic acid, a light-brown-colored chemical in bog water. Actually, tannin is harmless and has been used in folk medicine to treat tonsillitis and a variety of intestinal problems. During World War I, sphagnum moss, dripping with tannin, was used as a field dressing for wounds. Tannin is in tea; it is used to clarify wine and beer and in the tanning of leather. Although we were not interested in drinking water with a high concentration of tannic acid, and washing clothes in the stuff was out of the question, a shallow well was the only way we could afford water, and we went to talk it over with Ted and Louise.

"Where do you want your well?" Ted asked, working under the hood of his truck.

"I suppose in front of the cabin somewhere," I said, watching him skin his knuckles on a rusty nut. "You witched it yet?"

"Done what?"

"Witched it. You witched your place at all?"

"You mean have I walked around with a forked stick?" I laughed.

"I call it witching," he mumbled, still deep in the engine of his truck.

"You're kidding. You're telling me that you still use a water witch to find water?"

"It works." Ted reappeared and looked at me with his usual grin, only this time it was decorated with grease and oil. "I witched this here well—where you've been getting your drinking water."

Ted loved to pull our legs, and since we were greenhorns, he pulled longer and harder on us than on anyone we knew. When we first met him he told us that he had just been shopping for his wife for Christmas and had bought her a chainsaw. We hadn't met Louise yet, and didn't doubt him. "Had to," he said sadly, shaking his head. "She's been pulping out the back forty and busted the one I got her last year."

The next day Ted stopped by and we looked over the shape of the land surrounding our cabin. As usual, he didn't say much while he was working through a problem. We walked to a hill nearby and then down past the cabin and climbed the next rise. "You want your well over there, right?" He pointed to the southwest corner of the cabin.

"That's perfect," I said, growing curious about all our walking.

"Well, let's see what we got here," he said as we hiked down to the bog. He found a large healthy alder and, pulling a branch down, cut off a section that included a Y. I saw what he was up to

73

and laughed. He looked at me with a smile and began to whittle the thing into shape.

Soon we were back up by the cabin. He grasped the water witch with both hands, and began retracing the jaunt we had taken earlier. I snickered at the thought of this lengthy joke as we walked back the way we had come. After several turns in front of the cabin he announced that there were many veins of water running parallel to the structure and that we could pick any one we wanted.

"Your best bet is here," he said, holding the stick firmly and pacing slowly off the southwest corner. "It's closest to the place you wanted a well, and it feels strong."

"Ted, you're kidding me," I said, beginning to believe him.

"Watch me," he said. He walked across the yard, and the tip of the stick dipped once or twice. "You try it," he said.

I held the stick the way he had and began pacing perpendicular to the alleged veins of water. Nothing happened.

"Try it again," Ted said. I swatted at the mosquitoes and started across the yard. Once I thought I felt a slight tug, but I dismissed it. Meanwhile, Ted had scuffed out a small hole with the heel of his boot, marking the well site.

"I didn't feel anything," I said, disappointed.

"That's all right," he said, "but you ought to start digging here."

"Ted," I said, holding back my laugh until he smirked, "you aren't kidding, are you? I'm not going to dig some hole to China and then have you come back here and get a good laugh. It's too hot."

"Hey, I witch my wells, my dad witched his wells, Marty just witched a well, and now I've witched your well. There's water down there. Start digging." He lit a Pall Mall, shook his head, climbed into his pick-up, and left.

I stood there holding the water witch and looked at the heel prints in the gray clay. I held the stick as Ted had shown me and paced around the yard. I didn't feel a thing. I called to Jeanne, who had been inside all this time.

"Ted just witched water for us," I said.

Jeanne laughed. "Well, great. Why don't you bring in a pailful. I'm trying to do the washing."

"Why don't you try witching. He showed me how to do it."

Jeanne grasped the stick and walked around in circles.

"No," I said. "Go back and forth like this." I showed her where Ted had walked.

Jeanne made several passes and couldn't stop laughing. Then suddenly she stopped. "Oh, Dick! It's twitching, it's bobbing right here!"

I couldn't believe it. Jeanne was standing right over the spot that Ted had marked. "Are you kidding me?" I said, watching her eyes and the corners of her mouth. She was as serious as she'd ever been.

Assuming that I was not the victim of a crude conspiracy between Jeanne and Ted, I started digging.

I did this foul work knowing very little about the theory of it, and I often consulted with Ted. The idea was to get a length of pipe through the clay and roots and rock to a stream of underground water that traveled in a bed of gravel. Just how far down this bed of gravel was, no one knew for sure; but the strength of pull on the water witch had something to do with it. Ted thought we might find water at twenty-five feet. At the bottom end of the iron pipe we would install a heavy piece of screened pipe with a point. This sandpoint, or well point, was sensitive to heavy pressure, so I was digging a narrow hole through the tough stuff, the rock and clay, to prepare its way in search of the water.

"You want to dig down through all the clay until you start hitting gravel," Ted said one day while we discussed my slow progress.

"How far down do you think I'll have to dig?" I asked.

"Till you hit gravel," Ted said.

So I dug, first with a pickaxe to break the hardpan, then with a post-hole digger. I dug, I sweated, I slapped at mosquitoes. By the time I reached six feet and could no longer maneuver the post-hole digger, Ted appeared with a device that would take me deep into the unknown below. Again it was a length of pipe, but this time it had for a working end a pair of blades that looked very much like an electric fan. The idea was to lower this screw into the hole, twist it a turn and haul up several ounces of clay. As the auger worked its way into the earth, I would add lengths of pipe.

At first the little game was fun, but with each rock struck and worked slowly up the hole, I became less interested in a well and saw advantages in carrying water. I inspected each small pile of clay retrieved from the hole, looking for signs of gravel and water. More often than not, I spent an entire day trying to wrestle a single rock to the surface.

"You get yourself a big one in the path down there and you'll have to start all over again," Ted reminded me. "I've found a flat rock just above gravel. Damn, it makes a fellow mad."

"There's no other way?" I asked, brushing clay from my legs and arms and face.

"You can always have it drilled," Ted said.

A couple of weekend people down the road had decided against digging and hired a drilling outfit to find water. The rig pulled into the yard at daybreak and found water at three in the afternoon. They had bored two-hundred-fifty feet and charged the couple four-thousand dollars.

"We could put up two more cabins for that," Jeanne said. So I went outside, got down on my knees, and dug.

As I worked, local folks stopped by to watch and offer their advice. They stood with their backs to the sun as I searched my shovel for signs of gravel. Some would bend low and feel the texture of the clay and shake their heads. Others would pick up a recently dug rock and examine it with great concentration, searching their memories for bits of folklore to encourage me in my work.

"This here is basalt," one said. "Means you're getting close to gravel."

I noticed nothing unusual about the texture of my diggings, and my enthusiasm for the project waned in spite of the encouragement. Then one morning when I knelt before my digging machine, I saw that the hole was full of water. "Water!" I yelled so loudly that blue jays scattered and Jeanne dropped a dish inside the cabin.

She rushed outside, and together we stood looking at the brackish pool in the hole. "Is that what it's supposed to do?" she asked.

"I don't know. Let's see if it's any good."

I dipped a glass into the water and held it up to the sun. "Looks kinda dark," Jeanne said with the authority of a public health officer.

"We'll let it settle," I said.

The glass of brown water sat on our mantle for two days as we pondered its clarity. Finally, the silt settled, and the water was pure red-brown. I called Ted.

"Just a little surface water," he said, looking into the hole. "You'd better get it outa there."

"How?" I asked.

"Dip it out. Get me a coffee can." He dipped the coffee can into the hole, and after several scoops the water level went down an inch or so. "Yeah, it's just surface stuff," he said.

For a week I dipped the coffee can into the hole—first by hand, then by attaching the can to a long pole. Twice the can broke loose and sank to the bottom. I had to invent a tool to retrieve it, but finally I had scooped most of the water out and found that the bottom of the hole was covered with several feet of heavy, slimy mud. I dug the mud out one day, and that night it rained.

Jeanne woke me up that night. "Did you cover the hole?"

"Damn," I said, pulling on boots and going out to find a board to cover the hole. In the process of getting the board in place, I accidentally kicked a large rock into the hole and heard a distinct *ka-sploosh*.

We carried water in cans. We bathed carefully. Every drop of water did much work before it finally rolled down our legs and soaked into the ground. Often I glanced over at the boarded hole in disgust. Once I peeked and dropped the board back in place. The thing was full of water again. "You'd better clean it out," Ted said each time we saw him, which was more frequent as the summer heat demanded we consume more water.

"You get your well in yet?" they asked us in town.

One night near the end of July, after a long hot day at the museum, I kicked the board away from the hole and scooped water until it was dark. By lantern light I dug mud and rocks, and at sunrise I measured the depth of the hole: twelve feet.

Every night I dug. I fell on my knees and turned the pipe and stood up, pulling fifteen feet of heavy lead pipe and dumping out several ounces of clay. I reinserted the pipe, knelt in the cold clay, and one day produced a handful of gray gravel-like stuff. Ted came over right away. "How far you down?" he said.

"Eighteen feet," I replied, holding the coarse sandy material in my hand as though it were gold.

"Well, it's up to you," he said. "If you want to risk a sandpoint, we can try to hammer the thing down and see what you have."

"At this point I'd throw forty bucks down the hole if I thought it would do any good," I said, producing the shiny sandpoint that had cost Jeanne and me forty dollars.

"I'll stop by tomorrow. I've got some pipe, and we'll give it a try."

That night I didn't sleep well. I rolled around for hours in a light dream about Ted and me hammering length after length of pipe toward the center of the earth. I felt the give as the point collapsed under the weight of the hammer, and then I pulled until my arms ached to get the pipe out of the ground to try again.

Without our own water supply, Jeanne and I were kidding ourselves about living at the cabin for long. We could do very well without electricity; we didn't miss television or microwave ovens or any of the other conveniences that electric service provided. But

78

without water of our own, we were dependent upon our neighbors, and a big part of our coming to the woods was to reduce our dependency. Water, a well, was our greatest need.

After that restless night I met Ted in our yard. We drank coffee in silence, and then we collected our equipment and prepared to send the pipe and point down to find water.

"Look," Ted warned me, "if we hit a rock or plug the point up with clay or silt, we're going to have to pull it up. I just want to let you know that nothing's guaranteed. Okay?"

Nothing we had done in the woods thus far had been guaranteed, but Ted's warning bothered me. We could always pull up and try somewhere else, I thought as we hooked the heavy lengths of pipe together, but more witching and digging and dipping would put the prospect of having our own water supply far into the future.

"Tighten each joint," Ted said, flipping the monkey wrench to me. "We don't want the sections to fall apart down there."

Ted found a section of eight-inch pipe. We were going to use that as a casing for the water pipe. If we had to pull the point sometime in the future, there would be at least eighteen feet free and clear of the compacted clay. We dropped the assembled sections into the hole, and after connecting a drive pipe, Ted showed me how to tap the thing with a sixteen- pound maul. Slowly and with a steady rhythm he tapped the pipe, and the forty-dollar point disappeared into the gravel far below. As the length of pipe sank into the ground, we attached another.

"You keeping track of how many feet of pipe we got down there?" Ted said, smiling with a Pall Mall clenched between his teeth.

"About twenty, I think."

"You *think*?" His eyes widened. "Keep track of it." Ted tapped gently. Pall Mall butts began to collect in the soupy clay around us. *Tap...tap...tap.*

Thud. Ted dropped the heavy maul. He muttered something and picked up a flashlight. Lying in the muck, he peered into the hole. He muttered something else, and lighting another cigarette, he picked up the maul and gave the pipe a sharp blow. He tapped some more. The pipe inched its way down. Ted said, "Keep an eye on how much progress I'm making. Mark the pipe."

I made a line with a pencil near the point where the pipe went into the ground. Jeanne came out and stood nearby with her fingers crossed. *Tap...tap...tap.* I hadn't heard the sound of metal on metal in the woods before—a sharp crack that echoed in the trees. It was a cold, steely sound, the sound of permanent settlement. We were violating a section of land that hadn't been hammered before. We were hoping to puncture an underground stream that had been there when the land above was burning in the fire of 1894. The stream had been there when the Indians had hunted this land and told stories of white men in canoes on the St. Croix River. The stream had flowed through its gravel course even before the Indians arrived, and that day we were poking a steel point into its path hoping to interrupt its flow. *Tap...tap...tap.* Jeanne watched and crossed her fingers.

Ted put the maul down and sat back against the cabin. "How far we down?" he said, inspecting an empty cigarette package and feeling his shirt pocket for another.

"Well, your mark has gone down five inches, so we've got twenty-three feet and five inches below the surface," I said.

"If we don't get something soon you can trade your cistern pump in on a cylinder model," he said, drawing deeply on his smoke. "She'll only pull twenty-five feet, you know."

We had bought an inexpensive hand pump, a cistern pump. It pulled water up a pipe by vacuum, but twenty-five feet was the greatest distance it could pull. If the well was deeper than that, we would have to spend another hundred dollars on a pump with a cylinder that slipped into the pipe. If there was water down there, I didn't care how far we'd have to pull it. What worried me was that there might not be water down there at all. I wasn't sure that I believed in witching. But then how would I know? I'd grown up turning a faucet and watching water flow. Anything would surprise me now.

For another half hour Ted tapped the pipe. He knew that if he hit it too hard he might crush the point that was probing into hard gravel and then we would never know if there was water. He put the maul down and picked up the pail of water he had asked Jeanne to bring out. "If this works," he said, "we'll have something to put back in the pail. If it doesn't, we'll have a drink when you come over to get water tonight."

The idea was to pour water into the pipe. If it didn't fill up, the point was passing the water out into loose gravel. If there was loose gravel, we were near the underground stream. If the pipe filled, either the point was clogged or the point wasn't in gravel. The pipe filled up. My heart sank. Jeanne crossed her fingers tighter, and Ted picked up the maul and began to tap again.

A few moments later the maul seemed to jump up in Ted's hand. "We hit something," he said. He wiped the sweat from his face and gave it another rap. The maul jumped. He looked at me. "I'm gonna hit 'er hard. If it's rock, we might bust the point. If it's not rock, well...." I shrugged my shoulders. What good was a point if you didn't have water.

"Hit it," I said. Jeanne looked at me, and I thought to cross my fingers only to discover that they were already crossed.

With a great heave of the maul, Ted sunk the pipe at least six inches. The water that had been jiggling around in the pipe disappeared with a gurgle. Ted beamed. "Give me that pail!" he shouted. He poured water into the pipe and it all disappeared. Jeanne and I couldn't believe it. We held our breath while Ted screwed the hand pump onto the pipe. "Give me water!" he said as he pumped the handle madly. I poured water into the opening. Then, with an unlit cigarette dangling from his lips, he motioned me to step back.

A gush of brown water poured from the spout. I couldn't keep up with what was happening. Jeanne stared at the brown ooze. Ted pumped wildly. Slowly the brown color faded, and pure crystal clear water poured on the ground and into my boots. I stepped back and hugged Jeanne. "Water!" I said. "God, it's real water!" Jeanne jumped around and hugged Ted, who smiled, and, pumping slower, lit his Pall Mall with his free hand.

"All the water you can drink," he said. "Get a glass."

We pumped a shot into a glass, and Ted smelled it. He sipped it, and then Jeanne came out of the cabin with three wine glasses that we had saved from our city life. We filled the glasses and toasted Ted. We toasted the underground river and the sun. We even toasted the mosquitoes that had gathered for their usual afternoon feeding.

"Water!" I yelled. "I don't believe it."

Twenty-four feet, eight inches underground a prehistoric stream of cold water had been tapped. The point, buried in the ancient gravel, disturbed the flow, and the water ebbed around the point and charted a new river. We thought about that when we pumped our bath water that night.

8

The Shah of Iran had died of cancer in Cairo. Morning radio reports were saturated with news of coups, purges, riots, murder, and terror. President Carter's brother Billy was having an affair with Libya; the United States was breaking its date with the Olympic Games in Moscow. It seemed to Jeanne and me that the world was wobbling on its axis while we were enjoying the security of life in the woods and peace in our work at the museum. Our pace was slow and measured in a world where tense, unsure footsteps were followed by accusations and rifle fire.

One afternoon, when we returned to the cabin from our work, we skipped the evening news and instead went directly to the bog to look in on the cranberry crop. A low deck of ground fog had settled over the sphagnum fields, and we walked in a dream world of silence and rich smells. There was stability on a quaking bog in these troubled times. For thousands of years the fog had come to this place on cool August evenings; for thousands of years the loon had cried here and the cranberries had ripened on their low tangled vines. The spruce were smaller when the A-bomb erased Hiroshima. The dying birch on the ridge was but a weed during the Great Depression.

Through the gray shroud, Jeanne and I imagined the tall pine forests of another time. We imagined the loon's haunting cry and the deer moving ahead of an Indian hunter. We thought of the bear and the howl of wolves under the bright moon of autumn. The Chippewa man would have smiled at the wolfs call as he sat before his campfire, a flicker of light in the dense, dark forest. He too must have known the peace of this primeval place.

The loon cried again, *ha-oo-oot, ha-oo-oot*, and Jeanne and I stopped. We were shadows in the cool, damp mist. We could see neither shore of the bog; our vision was limited to a circle of ten feet. We were in the center of a pale dome, standing in a circle of bright green moss that rose high in fertile hummocks that reached out and touched our waists. We were elves in search of cranberries wet in the dew and hidden in the moss.

"Dick," Jeanne whispered as we often did when we were under the spell of the bog. "Look at these vines."

Tucked deep in their mossy beds were many small green berries on fragile vines dwarfed by bog rosemary and Labrador tea. These were the fruits of our soft, water-logged fields. Wild cranberries are small compared with the commercial varieties, but they are zesty tasting and a few went a long way to add relish to our Thanksgiving and Christmas dinners. Jeanne had even managed to make jelly from the left-over berries.

Ha-oo-oot. The loon cried, and we stepped forward, drawn by the bird and by the fog that cloaked the path ahead. The silhouette of a large black spruce grew darker as we approached, and we brushed against its wet branches in passing. Ahead, a big island rose suddenly from the sphagnum mat and disappeared into the dense fog.

We climbed the steep bank and walked into an ever-brighter world of birch and bracken fern until finally we had reached the summit and blue skies. There, we could see across the vast fog bank; we could see the tops of the spruce poking up from the opaque sea of cloud like small pines dotting an enormous field of fresh fallen snow. We stood there for a time as the sun, in its last hour, painted the fog bank pink and red, and at last the shadow of the western shore crept slowly across the field, leaving the fog gray and cold and wet.

We walked slowly down the steep bank; slowly into the colorless fog following a deer trail through the bog to the western shore of the woodlot. It was fast becoming dark, and we picked our path carefully. Nightsongs of birds and a chorus of frogs followed us to the high ground where the trail became narrow and thick brush pulled at us as we passed. We had been away from the cabin for several hours without a hint of the civilized world around us and we felt alone and walked arm in arm in the dark forest, stopping often to listen. A barred owl hooted. A male ruffed grouse drummed in his passion on a distant log. A deer moved behind us.

We were surrounded by creatures of the wood and bog, surrounded by life dependent on instinct for survival. We were the only mammals abroad that night armed with culture. We alone were operating under the rules of learned behavior, and just then it was a useless gift.

"Where are we?" Jeanne asked.

"I was just wondering that myself," I said, trying to recall something familiar in the dark woods around us. "I think the meadow is just over there." I wished we had stayed on the bog for our return trip. After a short hike off the trail we found no meadow, no landmarks.

"I think we've been going in a circle," Jeanne said. "I wish we'd brought the flashlight."

"A compass would have been handier," I said, sitting down on a log that sank slowly beneath my weight.

"I can't believe we can get lost on a hundred acres," Jeanne said, looking around at our brushy resting spot.

"I can," I said. "I was lost out here last week in broad daylight. There's a trail in here somewhere."

"Now you tell me. So what do we do?"

"Well, we can sit here and wait for a car to go down the county road. We'd know which way was west anyway. Or we can wait until the stars are bright, work our way to the bog, and follow the shoreline home. Or we can stay out here tonight and go back in the morning."

"We're going to get wet then," Jeanne said. "There's a storm coming." The ruffed grouse drummed again.

"I wonder if that's the grouse that hangs around the cabin. We know where his drumming log is. Why don't we follow the sound."

"It's hard to pinpoint it," I said. "We'd be walking all over the woods looking for the drumming log. Let's try to get to the bog. I think you're right about the rain."

For some time we stumbled through the bush without seeing much of anything, including fallen logs, which I managed to trip over frequently.

"Watch out for that log," I said, getting up.

"You're the one that's having the problem,"Jeanne laughed. "Have any idea where we are now?"

"Not the slightest," I said. I pulled a branch away from my face.

"Hey, look! This stump's been cut!" Jeanne said. "And here's a pile of logs."

"I cut that tree last week. We're on the east side of the ridge. The trail is on the other side of these logs."

We stepped over the woodpile and found ourselves in a clearing—the trail that led to the cabin. Jeanne was laughing again.

"We've been stumbling through a jungle, and all the time we were walking right next to the trail. Dumb!"

"Big-time woodsmen, eh?" I said, trying to imagine how we were able to get as far as we did in the dark forest. The grouse drummed again, this time far off to our right. I was glad we hadn't tried to follow that sound.

We lit the lamps in the cabin and quickly organized a dinner of cheese and bread. We were talking about the bog when automobile headlights flashed on the white birch trees outside.

I grabbed a kerosene lamp and went out onto the deck.

"Hello!"Ted shouted in the darkness.

"Come on in," I said, holding the lantern high, catching Ted and Louise in the yellow light. "We just got home from a walk."

"At night?" Louise said, laughing. "You could get lost out there."

"No problem," I said, glancing at Jeanne. "That's a nice branch you're wearing in your hair," Ted said, sitting down at the table.

I brushed the twig away and poured us all drinks. Jeanne turned the lamps low, and we sat back and chatted about people who had been lost on the bog and in the thick woods of these parts.

"What was that?" Jeanne said suddenly.

We all listened for a moment, then we heard it. Thunder.

"That's supposed to be some storm," Ted said. "It's knocked out power down in the cities."

We went outside to have a look. The southwest sky lit up brightly. "It's still a ways off, but I suppose we'd better get home and shut the windows," Ted said. "I've still got tools out, too."

We guided Ted and Louise to their car with our lanterns and watched their taillights disappear down the road. Soon the engine noise had faded and the rumble of thunder was closer. The air was still and muggy.

Jeanne and I had always liked storms in the city, but storms on the bog were different. They seemed much more violent, and we felt closer to their energy than we had in the city. The thunder shook the boggy ground, and the cabin shook with it. The lightning frequently struck trees on the place, and when it cracked overhead we could smell the ozone. The wind would bend the supple birch, and the tree tops sounded like whips snapping at a circus. We sat on the deck and drank tea and watched fireflies glow in the muggy air.

After a time a breeze came up and the first rain drops spattered in the clay of our front yard. The fireflies disappeared, cold air rushed in, and a crack of thunder sent us scurrying into the cabin to shut the windows. In a second the squall line hit us and the cabin was deluged; rain came at the small building from all sides. The thunder broke over the roof, shaking the dishes and sending a book down from the top shelf. The wind howled, the lightning strobed, and we turned the oil lamps down to watch the storm. We had the feeling that we were in a small boat on a heavy and difficult sea. We felt the cabin rise and fall as the birch flashed bright white in the lightning. The rain pounded so hard on the cabin roof that we had to shout to talk to one another. The front door blew open, and I propped a stick against the handle to keep it shut. A large branch hit the roof with a dull thump, and a bolt of lightning struck nearby with a bang and a trailing sizzle.

Then it passed. The thunder faded, the rains let up, the winds died. We sat in silence for some time, watching the lightning grow in the eastern sky, silhouetting the lean birch. The quiet was overwhelming. The sounds of the city always crept in behind a departing storm. Here, silence rushed in to fill the void. A spring peeper started the frog chorus at the pond, but the chorus broke off abruptly. To the south, another squall line was advancing. We slipped into bed to let its passage rock us to sleep.

By morning light we could see that the storm had done much work. Limbs lay strewn about, broken in their fall. Several tired aspen had split and fallen, and everywhere pools of water rested atop the hardpan. The radio news reports from the city could talk of nothing else. Thousands of homes had lost power, the streets had filled with water, trees were down everywhere snarling the morning traffic.

Armed with handsaws, Jeanne and I set out to collect the windfall for our stoves. The best kindling came from high dead branches of birch, and after any wind we could stack enough to last several months. We started on the driveway and discovered that the storm had knocked an old birch across the road. We hacked away on the big tree for some time before I finally returned to the cabin for our cross-cut saw. This tool was six feet long and had handles for two sawyers. We dragged the efficient blade across the birch until we had severed enough wood to get the car in and out. While Jeanne collected sticks I continued to work on the big tree, until Ted drove up.

"Lost a couple, huh?" Ted said, lighting a Pall Mall and looking down the length of the birch tree.

"Yeah, it'll make good firewood for Jeanne's cookstove," I said, happy to stop sawing for a time. "You lose any trees?"

"A couple. Say, what are you doing with a handsaw?"

I looked down at my saw wondering what I might be doing wrong. "Nothing, just sawing up this tree. Why?"

"Well, you got a chain saw, don't you?"

"Oh, yeah, but we never use the thing. Hell, this is good exercise, right?"

"You know how long it's going to take you to saw this birch into the little chunks you put in your stove? Let's warm up the chain saw."

I hesitated for a few minutes, and then I figured the time had come to learn how to use a chain saw. Jeanne's father had owned the tool in the city and used it to cut up storm damage. When we left for the woods he slipped it in the car thinking we might need it. Thus far, we had enjoyed cutting the windfall with handsaws.

There was music in the blade and great efficiency in the cutters and scrapers. It seemed compatible with our easy-going, quiet life. The chain saw, we thought, would be a noisy neighbor. Rattling and whining in deafening lunges, the chain saw tore into wood and sprayed dusty chips everywhere. Ted thought differently. "You can use your handsaws on the small stuff, but if you're planning to get wood up for the winter you'll have to use the machine. You and Jeanne'll be sawing from now until next spring just to stay even if you don't."

We dug the chain saw out of the shed, oiled it, and poured some gas into the small tank. With a single pull Ted had the thing screaming. The birds took off in a flurry, and Jeanne came running up the road. Ted smiled.

"Looks like you can use it to call the wife," he shouted over the roaring saw. Jeanne stood a distance away giving me threatening looks. She was covered with mud and holding her little Swede saw.

We walked down the road, and Ted started in on the big birch. In seconds he had made a cut and then another. I watched. It would have taken me ten minutes of steady cutting to lob off a piece of birch; in the same amount of time the chain saw whirred through the entire tree. I was beginning to see its advantages. Perhaps, I thought, I might do all my cutting at once—in one day—and then be done with it. That might not be so bad after all.

Ted showed me how to buck up a log and slice off chunks as easily as cutting butter. He showed me how to cut a log on the ground, roll it over and make a final cut. "Keep the chain away from the ground, or you'll be sharpening the blades more than you'll be cutting wood," he hollered. We walked into the woods, and he showed me how to fell a large tree with the saw. Using a cross cut, I could cut a notch and make a back cut in five minutes. With the chain saw, Ted toppled a dead tree in less than a minute. In the next four minutes he had cut the old aspen into stove-perfect chunks. Then he turned the machine off.

"There," he said. "All ready for Jeanne to split. Now you try it."

He handed me the saw and pointed to a dead, leafless birch, and I began a notch, thinking that the racket would get me before the chain broke. The notch made, I began a back cut. Ted poked me. "Always look around before you drop a tree," he shouted. I had forgotten. With a handsaw there was plenty of time to study the fall before I came even close to felling a tree. With the chain saw it all happened so fast that I almost dropped the tree without looking. I looked, the saw vibrating in my hands, then I pressed the blade into the cut and the tree came down with a thump. Carefully I began a series of cuts along the trunk the right size for our stove and then kicked the log over and finished the cut on the other side. It was done. I switched the saw off and waited for a moment until I could hear again.

"Coffee?" I said.

When Ted left that afternoon, I went deep into the woods and began sawing fallen timber. I couldn't believe how easy it was to slice up a few wheelbarrow loads in just minutes. But when I turned the machine off and sat on a stump to take a break I knew something was missing. Something had passed with the inefficiency of my handsaw. It was the gentle grating sound, the small, neat pile of sawdust, the awareness of life on the woodlot around me as I worked. With a handsaw I could hear the cracking of a twig and look up to see a deer watching. I could stop sawing in an instant to watch a flight of wood ducks pass overhead. As my Swede saw sliced through the trunk of a tree, I could contemplate the growth rings and imagine the history as my blade passed through the years of the tree's development.

I rested often with a handsaw. I absorbed the woodlot. It was happy work, quiet work. Not so with my newly activated chain saw. It tore angrily into history, ripping away the years. It whirled the chips of wood into a lashing sea of dust that settled in a great pool around the fatal cuts. The sound echoed across the bog, and all of the natural world passed above me, passed far to my flanks without my slightest notice. It was a wood-cutting machine. Its purpose was efficiency, and it didn't give a hang about my relationship with nature.

When I had cut enough wood to see us comfortably through the remaining summer and deep into the fall, I returned to the cabin with aching forearms and a heavy heart. The practical business of living in the woods was for the first time at odds with my enjoyment of the place. I had probably produced more firewood that afternoon than I had in all the time that we had lived at the cabin. But I had not felt the effects of the woodlot as I did during my more primitive wood-gathering days. I felt a slave to production with the chain saw, and the purpose of our being in the woods escaped me for a time.

"I think you're making too much of it," Jeanne said. "You don't have to use the machine."

"But don't you feel kind of silly living our romantic dream when all around us efficient tools are available?"

"Of course not," Jeanne said, slicing a loaf of fresh-baked bread. "If we had come here to cut wood, we would have used a chain saw from the beginning. We came here to live simply, but that doesn't mean we can't use whatever resources are available if we want to. We aren't trying to live authentic nineteenth century or anything like that. Use the saw when you want to, chop with an axe when you want to. We aren't trying to prove anything."

Of course we weren't. What we were doing was living as simply as possible, adding tools as we needed them. I began to see what had bothered me. My inclination in the past was to buy an abundance of tools and then wander around looking for some use for them. Here, we had started with nothing and added conveniences as we found utility for them. What we were trying to avoid was collecting paraphernalia that added little to our enjoyment of life.

The chain saw had a place in our lives because we consumed a lot of wood. Like the car and the telephone and the well, the chain saw made it possible for us to get along with the twentieth century, while living in a primitive cabin close to nature. I found that I could get up a year's wood supply in a week of work. We still went out with handsaws in search of kindling, but the bulk of our fuel was cut and stacked and ready to split. At a time when home heating oil and natural gas had increased in price so dramatically, we were glad to have heaping piles of firewood at the ready for the winter to come.

"I feel like it's our savings account," Jeanne said one afternoon as we hiked by a stack of birch. "In fact, I feel more secure about a cord of firewood than I do with money in the bank."

Much of what happened in August increased our feelings of security. The garden produced beautiful tomatoes, which Jeanne canned. We dug a root cellar for the potatoes and carrots and beets. The bean crop far exceeded our needs, and we traded our surplus for corn.

As baskets of produce appeared on the deck of the cabin and Jeanne's pressure cooker rattled happily on the cookstove, we felt a sense of security that we had never known before. We could survive by our wits and by our sweat at a time when many families in the country were becoming neurotic with the fear of being left behind in the dust of inflation and shortages of food and fuel.

9

The bright setting sun shined on the towering cloud of a large retreating thunderstorm, exaggerating its somber tone; the birch trees stood tall and hard and white against the blue-black backdrop of rain. Golden leaves fell heavy with moisture and empty of life. The storm had been noisy, with much cool air on its heels, a welcome breeze that stirred the forest vapors and gave us our first rich smell of fall.

It was September when I had first seen the bog. I was flying a small airplane north from the Twin Cities to an early morning meeting in Duluth. Just at sunrise, I happened to look down to see the first warm rays of sunshine across the bogland below. The texture of the sphagnum mat was soft and fine like a carpet, but broken by many small islands and groves of black spruce. There was little evidence of settlement; the high ground appeared dense in aspen and birch. I circled the spot on my map.

Late that afternoon, on my return trip, I found the bog again and, reducing the power of the single engine Cessna, I dropped down low over the ancient lake to have a good look. The islands drifted slowly beneath my wings; the air was calm, and the roar of my engine seemed muted, far away. I turned the plane and followed the contour of the woodland shore. Birch trees shimmered pale white in the fading sunlight. I looked overboard from side to side and saw nothing that suggested life. There was mystery below me in the deep shadows that rushed under the plane from all sides.

There was loneliness here, and I felt a chill as another island loomed before me, out of the mosses, into my view. I turned to the south, dipping a wing over the blazing red cranberries, and then I saw the deer. There were eight of them in single file along a narrow trail that connected one island to another. They were frozen, watching the plane, as I pulled away. I longed to walk in that place, and I advanced the throttle. The plane climbed into the sunset, and I marked my map again.

A month later I sat in the front seat of the realtor's car as we bumped along the rough gravel road. We passed small farmsteads carved from brush and rock and surrounded by marsh. We passed hunting cabins set deep in birch woodlots; red shacks trimmed with white and swallowed by the bracken fern. Often we passed a lone stand of white pine; tall and shaggy guards on empty plains. Finally we pulled over on the side of the road and stopped.

"There you be," the realtor said, pointing to a wall of stark white birch trees that stood knee-deep in hazel and tangles of vine and grasses, long dried and brown. The luster of summer had departed the place, but the woodlot gleamed red and yellow in its autumn colors. "There's an old logging road over there if you want to walk in a ways," said the realtor.

What remained of the road was covered with brush, but I could see where the cut had been made by the loggers. Deer had long possessed the trail and it had grown narrow by their use. There was still the faint smell of sweet fern in the cold, moist air, and a ruffed grouse exploded from the dogwood in front of us.

"There's good bird hunting in here," the realtor said, catching his breath. "The oldtimers around here tell me that they used to hunt deer up there on that rise." We pushed through the thickets and gained higher ground. Stands of birch, white in the fading light, rose above us as we climbed the ridge. Fields of bracken fern standing tall as our waists rocked gently in the cool breeze that penetrated the woodlot. A large crow circled above the forest canopy, cawing with a strong voice that echoed on the distant shore. The bogland lay before us.

"There's a good bit of swamp out there, and part of it is on this property," the realtor said grimly. "I just want to be sure that you know that."

"That's perfect," I said. "It's a bog, isn't it?"

"I don't know what you call it, but it's wet and you can't do much with it," he said. "I'll tell you one thing, though: I wouldn't go out there. A fellow wants to be careful about this swampy ground."

We walked to the edge of the bog. A marsh hawk soared low across the mat through the yellow tamarack and into the grove of spruce, a black smudge on the distant shore. At my feet, pools of dark water reflected the pale orange sky above and hid the long, dead grasses beneath the surface. I reached down to wet my hand and smell the rich flavor of this still water. The realtor gave me a suspicious glance, and we turned to walk back to the car.

As we hiked down the ridge we passed bushes of blackberries, the plants of wild strawberry, and tall pin cherry trees. Alder was growing in thick stands on the shore of the bog, aspen crowded the trail, and here and there were pools of standing water with cattail and marsh grass. Every few feet the plant life changed as we gained higher ground and then dropped down in low gullies.

"This is wild land, and that's about it," the realtor said. "If that's what you're looking for, I mean."

"It's perfect," I said, ducking under a low-hanging branch covered with lichen. I stopped to inspect the growth, and my companion buttoned his jacket.

"It sure gets cold down here in the afternoon,"he said. We pushed on through the brush toward the road.

When we broke out of the woods the sun had set and the full moon would rise in a few minutes. I stood on the road and watched as the golden orb lit the sky behind the spruce and rose above the bog. Then we drove away. Later that night, after I signed the papers for the land, I went home and dreamed. Sitting in my chair overlooking the city lights, watching cars move slowly across a bridge, I dreamed about the lichen hanging from the branches of the dying thorn tree. I dreamed about the aspen leaves quaking in the breeze and the brown grasses that rattled underfoot. I thought of the crow that circled and cawed in a husky voice, and then I slept.

The cloud bank moved eastward, and the sun sank below the horizon. An airplane droned high overhead. Four years had passed since I had seen the bog on that early morning flight. Four years of work in the city, four years of life in the mainstream. We had visited the bog often in those years. We had picked flowers, planted trees, and photographed the birds and the deer and the fog at sunrise. We had watched crab spiders change their coloration and ride daisies in the wind. The spiders were waiting for insects as we were waiting for an idea: How could we arrange our lives so that we might come to the woods to live?

From the cockpit I had thought it a dream to live in the woods. Now, standing with my axe on the forest floor watching someone's small plane fade away to the south, I felt an emptiness that often comes with the realization of a dream. We had worked hard to achieve simplicity, we had given up much to enjoy the peace of the woodlot. The emptiness, the bare spot that remained when our dream became a reality, was filling with a sense that was foreign to us, a sense of the natural world, a sense of the wild. Our pleasures were in the birth of a flower, in the seed scattered by the wind and fed by the rains. Our pleasure was in the egg left by the ovenbird in a trailside nest, an egg that may be food for the skunk or hatch and carry the genes another generation more.

Our love for each other grew out of a new-found respect for one another's abilities to contribute to the whole of our life. Our world was stronger and more meaningful because of the presence of each other. At a time when world powers were shouting threats of nuclear build-ups, we felt privileged to live in the midst of the rocks and roots and primal ooze on which life depended. It was clear to us that the potential for world destruction was very great. Men and their ideologies were in conflict, and their technological abilities to make war seemed to outstrip their diplomatic prowess. Four and a half-billion years ago the earth may have begun with a bang. What difference would it make to our galaxy if the earth should flare bright one day and dissolve into dust? What difference if the skunk should eat the ovenbird's egg?

In the light of dusk I filled my wheelbarrow with split birch and worked my way to the main trail back to the cabin. Looking up I saw, at some distance, Jeanne's white cap bobbing in the gray light. She appeared and disappeared as she moved down the trail. Hidden by the great aspens and diffused as she passed through a hillock of pin cherry, she hiked ever closer, yet the distance between us did not seem to close.

Only once in a great while did we realize the true course of our trails. Each trail wandered about the woodlot like a meandering stream, touching the red oak and shooting off to the right where the woodpecker tree invited a turn to the left down to the pond where the spring peepers are likely to begin their spring chorus. We had cut the trails in the summer when the brush was dense, but our enthusiasm was strong. Down on our knees, we clipped away the hazel and the dogwood and inspected the rocks and the mushrooms revealed in our cutting. It was not an efficient way to make trails— armed with clippers and field guide and compass—but we were more interested in what our cuttings would uncover than where the trail would lead. We built the paths to take us to firewood, and firewood is everywhere. So are our paths.

In the failing light I could see Jeanne ahead, dwarfed by the tall birch, kneeling to inspect some small bush. I pushed the loaded wheelbarrow to her side, and she turned from the dogwood plant.

"We have new neighbors," she said.

"Neighbors?"

"Larry and Moe," Jeanne laughed. "Two deer mice have discovered our corn storage in the shed. You have to see it."

We hiked slowly back and stacked the birch on the deck of the cabin. Jeanne led me to the shed where inside a large can that contained corn for the animals were two very fat deer mice. They were chewing contentedly and took no notice of us peering into their lunchroom.

"I found them in here this morning," Jeanne said, "so I put this stick in for them to crawl out. Watch." She picked up a long stick and dropped it into the can. The mice ran up the stick, ran along the edge of the can and jumped to the handle of a nearby shovel. Down the shovel to the floor and through our legs they trotted. One of them went out the door, the other one stopped. He looked up at us for a moment, and then he turned and retraced his path back to the corn. Inside the can again, he picked up a kernel of corn and hastily repeated the evacuation to rejoin his friend.

"I think they've been eating our corn all along,"Jeanne said. "But as the level of corn went down, I guess they couldn't jump back out."

"Larry and Moe, eh?" I said, trying to register two more names on our growing list.

The next morning I followed Jeanne to the shed. The deer mice were there, huddled together after a long night of feasting. Jeanne dropped the stick into the can, and the mice climbed out. They looked at us with wide dark eyes and slid down the shovel, homeward bound.

Every morning Jeanne followed the same routine before she filled the birdfeeders, and I could hear her greeting the mice as I built a fire in the cook- stove. Finally, the containers needed refilling, and the mice were able to get along on their own until the level was once again too low for them to manage without the stick. Larry and Moe were with us for some time before Jeanne came into the cabin one morning and announced that Moe was missing. He remained on the missing list, and one day Larry was gone, too.

The cabin mouse didn't have a name. She was a white-footed mouse who had arrived in a hurry late in August to build a brooding nest. We met her one evening while we were reading and she was running from shadow to shadow with a mouthful of paper. She ran under the stove and waited. Then she ran to the cupboard and up the wall into a crack. Listening carefully, we could hear her in the ceiling. In a few minutes she would appear again under the stove, then scurry across the rug and into the wastebasket. She worked only after dark, and as she grew accustomed to us she collected her materials closer and closer to our reading chairs.

After we had gone to bed we listened to her travel about the cabin far into the night. When the nest was completed she seemed to calm down and often visited the window near our bed. She would sit for hours on the sill looking out through the screen. As the night air became cooler and we shut the window at bedtime, we always had to check for her and many times coax her back into the room.

One night I looked up from my book to see her at my elbow on an end table. She was perched on a stack of books, staring at me with beady little eyes.

Then she pulled a length of dried flowers from a vase and scampered off. We didn't see her for several days, and then one night, when I had stayed up late to do some writing, I happened to see four small mice scaling the wall over the front door. Suddenly, one of the mice lost his grip and fell to the floor with a loud splat. Sure that I was going to have to clean up a dead mouse, I approached the creature with a dustpan. I picked him up and cradled him in my hand. Although he couldn't have been more than a day or two old, he was fat and full bodied and in every way a white-footed mouse. In a moment he stirred, and I held him close to the wall, which, after a second to clean a foreleg, he scaled with no difficulty. The mice stayed in the cabin for another day, and then they left.

Jeanne and I had never given much thought to the notion that animals and birds could make errors in their judgment. We had always assumed that their behavior was so coded and their highly specialized abilities so expert, that any mistake was certain death.

But one morning Jeanne noticed a small sharp-shinned hawk perched uncomfortably on a feeder. He was pinned to the box in fear although there appeared to be nothing wrong with him physically. What was odd was that the blue jays, who usually sounded the alarm when a hawk was anywhere near the woodlot, were quiet. What was even more curious was the great number of jays at the corn pile only a few feet away from the hawk. We watched. The hawk was frozen. Suddenly the hawk pushed off the feeder and climbed up through the canopy of the birch trees. The blue jays went wild. They started a chorus of their hawk call, switched to the intruder call they used when someone came to visit us, and ended the confusion by calling for an assembly. When most of the jays had quieted down they flew off into the trees to roust the hawk. Oddly, the hawk had remained near the cabin and was now faced by a gang of screaming blue jays. The hawk left his high perch and chased a single jay until the others arrived to help. The aerial duel lasted for five minutes, and then the hawk flew off to the west. For the rest of the morning the jays chattered about the adventure. No matter what bird came to the feeder, the hawk call went out and the jabbering began.

We have seen the jays use the hawk call many times to take advantage of the feeders. The call is taken seriously by all birds and animals in our yard. Even the deer are likely to pause in their feeding and watch for the incoming hawk when the alarm is sounded. Squirrels, chipmunks, redpolls, finches, juncos, and chickadees all scatter when the blue jays have spotted a hawk. When the pressure on the feeders is too great for the jays to feast with ease, we have noticed that they will disappear for a moment and suddenly begin the hawk call. When all the squirrels and birds have taken cover, the jays glide in to the feeders. It doesn't seem to matter how often the jays cry hawk, the yard invariably empties when a new call is issued. When the hawks do come into the yard, they are usually successful in their work. We have seen a rough-legged hawk approach the woodlot and move from tree to tree—unseen by the jays—until he is directly over the feeding stations. In a flash he is in the midst of the smaller birds and away with a victim before the jays sound the alarm.

A kill in the yard seldom interrupts the feeding frenzy for more than a few minutes, however. Although the strike is a shock to the serenity of the setting and the jays seem to worry about it for hours, life soon returns to normal and many pounds of sunflower seeds are quickly reduced to dust.

We had lived on the woodlot for six months as September began, and in that time the novelty of the woods and our primitive lifestyle had become routine. We found that the living was easy and peaceful. Jeanne enjoyed cooking on her woodstove far more than she had on the electric model we used in the city. She had produced bountiful dinners and stores of breads and cakes and cookies and pies. Pumping water by hand, walking to the outhouse, heating with wood and reading by kerosene light all seemed natural and right. Living together in a single room, sixteen by twenty-four feet, forced us to practice cooperation, and our relationship was warmer than it had ever been before. We didn't perceive that we were doing without; we understood, instead, that we had lived with excess before we moved to the woods. With little high-value property to guard, to insure, or to worry about, we were becoming free. Free to set off on a morning hike to collect berries, free to camp on an island, free to sit in the bush for hours and watch a herd of deer browse in the dogwood.

If anything troubled us after our first six months on the place, it was the complexity of the outside world. We feared that an unhappy people with wounded pride would unleash a nuclear war. At a time when we had discovered prosperity in the simple life, it seemed the world was searching for happiness in greater consumption—and was finding instead hate enough to destroy the earth.

10

There was no color in the forest under the light of the harvest moon, only shapes, brilliantly lit, crisscrossed by sharp, cold, black shadows that spilled across the forest floor of damp leaves and into voids where there seemed to be nothing at all. It was the night of the hare, the barred owl, the coyote, and the sadness of summer's death. The sun had crossed the celestial equator, and the nights grew long in their hours; at first as long as the day, then longer. The oil lamps in our windows shined into the night fog that rose from the sphagnum and climbed the banks of alder and snaked like smoke around the cabin. We dressed warm for our moonlight walk, because the air, though still, was cold and wet.

As we followed the trail back into the woods and down into a gully where the fog lay heavy and gray among the fallen trees, I thought about a survivor's account of the Hinckley fire that I had read at the museum. It was the story of an escape from the forest fire that had occurred not far from our land. It was Frank Haney's story.

On Saturday, September 1st, 1894, Frank and a couple of his friends were preparing to leave their Kettle River campsite in search of cranberries. It was a hot, dry day, and the smell of smoke was in the air: "It was probably after two o'clock and getting smoky. We all went into the office and sat reading some books, waiting for the others to get back from the river. I was the first to notice how dark it was getting. I went outside and stood looking at the river. Then I saw the tops of high leaping flames and heard Tom Corbett yell. He was running up the short cut trail to tell us the fire was crossing the river."

Frank and his friends jumped into action. They loaded a wagon with blankets, food, an axe, and moccasins.

"Wilson and Chris got the team out and hitched up in record time and away we went with Chris up front lashing the horses, Tom lying flat facing forward hanging onto the sides of the box; moccasins and shoepacs flying out on the rough spots, and Wilson and myself in the rear. I had my shotgun and Wilson was carrying a gun that Tom had brought up from the river. We had a good piece of road for about a mile or more across a jackpine plain. It was straight and smooth for a wood's road, but in spite of the best Chris could do with the team, the fire was right up close and gaining. Wilson said, 'Frank, I'm going to hang onto this gun and shoot myself if I have to die.' I made up my mind to do that myself and kept it in my mind all the way."

It was then that the men came to a stand of virgin pine and had to leave the wagon. The thick forest of tall pine had slowed the fire, but the smoke was heavy.

"While they turned the team loose I was groping for a pool of water in the [dry creek bed]. I couldn't see as the clouds of black smoke shut off the light so completely that the only way to avoid running into the trees was looking ahead and up where there was a red reflection against the sky and we could see the bodies of the trees against it. Trying to find water to get into without being able to see, I tangled in the brush. I yelled to the others to keep straight ahead. I think that was the only time Tom Corbett was right with the others. It was so dark I couldn't see him there. He was about fifty years old and the pace was too hot. I was in the lead again, and when I knew we were losing contact with Tom, I fired one shot, then realized that that wouldn't help as some of the trees that were breaking around us sounded like gunshots. I had on heavy river driver shoes and when one of the laces came loose I cut the other one with my hunting knife, kicked the shoes off and threw the knife and belt away. My socks soon flew off and from then on until I found some discarded rubbers the next day, where a camp burned, I was barefoot."

The men were now under a crown fire. The tops, or crowns, of the pine trees were ablaze, and the pitch-laden air exploded as the wind of the fire whipped the tall trees sending burning branches down on the men below.

"Some tops fell around us, one right in front of me. They scattered the fire, but no one got hit—unless it was Tom, we didn't find his body. We came out of the timber onto O'Neal's tote road that paralleled Sand Creek. We turned south and were now running with the fire close to our right-hand side. Then, before I got into good light, I struck a projecting knot on a log with my left knee so that it stopped me. Wilson bounded by me.... Hobbling along behind him, I saw the logging road that ran downgrade directly away from the fire, to what was probably the best place we could have found if given lots of time. I called Wilson back. Chris was playing out but got there to see us turn down the log road and followed it calling to us to save ourselves if we could. He was all in and couldn't go much further."

Frank and Wilson ran along a wide road with Chris some distance behind them. Slash from the logging operations was burning on both sides of the road. Then through the smoke they saw a creek. They ran back and helped Chris and got him into the water just in time. The fire was nearly upon them.

"When we were in the water and Wilson saw what was coming he said, 'I don't think we can stand it in here.' I felt the place was perfect. There was a green grassy bank a little more than two feet high above water level and nearly two feet of water right up against the bank. There was plenty of room for the three of us side by side. There was some skids lying on the bank. I thought to guard against anything heavy blowing in on us I would lay the skids above us across the creek. I only had time to place one of them when I had to jump back in. Forty feet downstream a bunch of deer jumped across. Wilson was holding a heavy wool sock over his mouth with his left hand and keeping the air full of water, splashing with his right.

"Just as the blast swept the tall timber clean that bordered the creek bottom, I ducked under with my woolen overshirt pulled up over my head so that when I came up for air, I got it through wet cloth. That worked perfect. The others had some trouble and did some coughing. When the blast struck, the water was sizzling with fire brands. The fish died quick. A rabbit swam against me and I broke its neck and threw him on the sandbar with my gun which came through okay except for a scarred stock."

When the firestorm had passed, Frank had another surprise. His dog, which he hadn't seen during the run, was in the water by his side, its nose shoved up under the bank. Frank, Wilson, and Chris crawled up on the sandbar and waited until morning to return to their camp.

Jeanne and I walked carefully among the stumps submerged in the fog and found a resting place on the ridge. We had often come to the ridge to listen on such a night, and as the moon rose and the shadows grew shorter, a chorus of coyote songs reached us from far off on the bog. We sat together for a long time. The fog rolled in off the bog and drifted through the ravine below the ridge. The coyotes' voices trailed off into the night. Not far from where we sat, Frank Haney and Wilson and Chris had waited in the September night for the smoke to clear and the earth to cool. They must have talked about Tom Corbett in low voices, about the death of the logging industry around Hinckley, but they couldn't have known how much death there had been that night. Four-hundred square miles of timber was gone, six villages were gone, and, like Corbett, four-hundred-and-eighteen people died that night in east-central Minnesota.

"Are you still thinking about Frank Haney's story?" Jeanne asked.

I nodded and said, "It's our land now, but I keep thinking that Frank may have been here, on this ridge, on a night like this, filling his pipe and listening to the coyotes."

Jeanne said, "I know, I get those feelings sometimes when I'm feeding the birds. I think: I'm feeding the descendants of chickadees that ate the bread crumbs of loggers who had their lunch right here on the ridge." Jeanne's voice seemed far away. "We still have our dream, though," she said. "We still have our years to live on this place. It's ours to use in our time."

For a while we sat in silence, watching the changing forms shaped by the drifting fog and lit by the moon. A hill that seemed far across the bog suddenly moved closer, and a barred owl swept low over the ridge and then away out of sight. The chill had penetrated our jackets when we finally rose and started back down the trail. A lamp in the window beckoned us. A yellow smear in the fog bank ahead beckoned us from the cold, damp mists into the warm cabin where hot tea waited. The coyotes began another song.

One morning, early in October, after we had pumped our bath water, Jeanne announced that she had been working on plans for a sauna. It surprised me because I too had been making sketches for a similar addition to our place. We had been enjoying our easy, serene sponge baths on the deck. There was nothing quite like them. Gathering the materials for a bath, heating the water to the right temperature, standing naked in the sun were all part of the drama that concluded with a rest in a large terrycloth robe in a lawn chair. It took a long time to prepare the bath, and, depending upon the weather, it took a long time to bathe. So we never rushed the ritual, we let it unfold and catch us up in its magic. We discovered a curious improvement in our skin condition. There was no need for lotions when the body was allowed to produce its own oils. We no longer suffered dry skin, nor the tight, uncomfortable feeling that came with daily showers in the city. We had released our bodies from the bondage of the scrubbing and gave our skin a chance to breathe.

The sauna would simply be an extension of that kindness. The dry heat of a Finnish sauna opened pores and let the inside out, so to speak. A true dry sauna was relaxing to sore muscles, a solace to cluttered minds, and the perfect end to a long day in the woods.

"We'll be closing the museum for the season at the end of this month, so we'll have time to build it before the snows," Jeanne said, happily producing her building plans. "I think it has to be small, just big enough for you and me, with a little woodstove."

"That's what I figured," I said, digging through a pile of papers for my drawings. "About six feet square with a sheet-metal stove. What do you think about building it on the east side of the garden?"

"So far from the cabin?"

"I think the walk will be nice. Besides, the garden will be the best place to take a snow bath since there's no brush in there. Also, I think we'd better remember to keep outbuildings away from the cabin in case we have a fire."

We walked around the garden several times and picked a fairly level spot. With brush knives we cleared the area and then stood back to inspect our future bath house.

"I can feel the winter sun already," Jeanne said. "Let's stake it out."

We marched around the clearing, pacing out six feet.

"Is that six feet inside or outside?" Jeanne asked, holding a foot in the air while waiting for my answer.

"I don't know, I haven't built it yet," I said, standing in the center of the plot, admiring the view to the east.

The saunas that Jeanne and I had experienced in the past were for the most part disappointing. In the city we often found large rooms lined with tile for efficient cleaning and big electric stoves that strained to heat the room to one-hundred-fifty degrees Fahrenheit. People arrived and departed the sauna with much chatter, opening and closing the door and letting heat go out in their passing. Even more annoying was the bather who was forever pouring water on the rocks until they ceased to sizzle. It was the bather's mistaken belief that steam did the work of the sauna bath.

Actually, bathing in a Finnish house in northern Minnesota, one discovers that tranquility is the watchword and dry heat the working force of the bath. There is no chatter, no running in and out, and certainly no dousing of the rocks until the very end of the bathing ritual. The dry heat opens pores and lets the body sweat profusely. Then the bather may step outside and cool off with a cold plunge into a lake, or, in the winter, by rolling in deep snow. Returning to the sauna, the bather again sweats, relaxes, and achieves a feeling of peace. The process is repeated until the very end, when a small amount of water sprinkled on the rocks produces an intense steam that serves as a final bath. Afterward, wrapped in a towel, the bather should find a warm room in which to relax. The last rest gives the body a chance to slowly regain normal temperatures. Such a process is almost impossible in a public sauna where so many notions and philosophies and needs must bathe together.

Our sauna would be private and hot and relaxing. If we were careful, we wouldn't burn it down. All I had to do now was find a source of lumber—and that gave us the excuse to have chocolate cake with Ted and Louise.

"Sure, I know where a fellow can get some popple cheap," Ted said, licking frosting from his fingers.

"Great! Where?" I said.

"Right here," he replied.

Ted and Louise were building a new home far back on their property, and Ted figured that he would have a lot of aspen boards left over when he finished the house. It was rough-cut lumber just as we had used to finish the interior of our cabin.

"I'll have plenty of wood for you by the end of October, if you can wait," Ted said.

"Perfect timing," Jeanne said. "We'd like to start building as soon as we close the museum."

"Getting tired of taking baths in dishpans, eh?" Louise said, bringing a plate of fresh cake to the table. "But you'd never get me in one of those sauna baths."

"It's going to take some wood to burn," Ted said. "Are you sure you have enough for the winter?"

That troubled me. A couple of days earlier I had noticed that despite my careful planning, my picturesque stacks of firewood were dwindling fast. Jeanne had done some extra canning of tomatoes, which she had been given by a neighbor, and nights in late September and early October had been colder than normal. Now, planning for a sauna, I could see that we were going to need a great deal more wood than I had cut and stacked. When we returned to the cabin that afternoon, I set out on the trails to inventory our supplies.

By the time I reached the ridge, I realized that we were in serious need of firewood. We had been burning nearly a tree a week during September. If we conserved, the wood on hand would last until December. With a sauna, we wouldn't make it through November. I had heard stories of people running out of cut and dried firewood and spending several hours a day through January and February foraging for burnable material. In those cold months, once a fellow gets behind he stays behind, Ted had told me. "You can run out of food for a week in January, but you'd better have wood to burn," he'd said.

I hiked into the brush to look for fallen aspen. Aspen, or "popple" as it's called in the country, is considered low on the scale of efficient firewood. It is a soft wood that burns rapidly and has the heat value of a sack of Popsicle sticks. Nevertheless, we had a lot of it on the woodlot and it was easy to collect. If I started hauling it in right away, we might be able to conserve our dried birch for the coldest months.

While I was potting about among the aspen, I heard a series of bird calls that were familiar, but I couldn't quite match the sound to a name. It troubled me because it was a glad sound, and until Jeanne came running down the trail with news that the evening grosbeaks had returned, I hadn't realized how close we were to the end of October.

Evening grosbeaks always returned to our feeders from their breeding grounds in Canada and Upper Michigan during the last week in October. While we were weekend campers we had watched them and fed them sunflower seeds until they returned to the Far North late in April. Always faithful to their schedule, these large yellow and black finches foretold the coming of cold nights and snow. Without fail, they arrived on the feeders at eight in the morning, retired to the treetops by ten, returned at noon, and were away by mid-afternoon. Their huge conical bills were most effective in cracking sunflower shells, and our usual party of fifty birds managed to devour five pounds of seeds a day.

The grosbeaks were a cheerful lot to have around the place. They got on well with the other birds and squirrels, chatted continuously with each other, and brought much color to a drab forest awaiting the first snowfall. In the morning, when I went into the woods with the wheelbarrow to collect wood, many of the grosbeaks followed, finding a suitable tree near my work in order to superintend my efforts. Around the cabin they acted as guards, warning us of approaching visitors. When a car came up the drive, the grosbeaks would take flight in a loud explosion of wings and shrieks, upsetting the blue jays and the squirrels who would all join the chorus. Most visitors took note of this activity and were quite nervous about it all until the menagerie had quieted down.

"How do you keep all those birds here?" a neighbor once asked.

"Actually, they keep us here," Jeanne said. "We're their prisoners."

There was some truth in that. Fifty pounds of sunflower seeds cost us about twelve dollars, and when the feeders were empty the birds flew to the treetops and started a ruckus that we could hear far back in the woods. One of us would hurry in our work and rush back to the cabin to restock the feeding platforms.

"Why bother?" the neighbor asked. "That's an awful expense just to keep a few birds around."

The birds and the animals that hung around the cabin were the chief reason we lived here. We often talked about the purpose of our life in the woods, and we always agreed that we were here to watch. The seeds and corn that we spread in the yard was bait, in a sense, to attract wildlife to our corner of the forest. Always, when we looked out our windows, there was something going on. Whether there were crows, jays, rabbits, deer, raccoons, bear, or a flock of juncos, we were always able to watch the wildlife interact.

And there was more to it than that. The creatures that had made our yard a part of their lives had come to trust us. It was possible for Jeanne and me to walk in the woods and have animals at our feet. We didn't contrive to make pets of them, and we didn't want to hold them; we wanted to establish a relationship of trust in our refuge. We wanted to be able to observe wildlife in nature. The only cage on the place was our cabin, and we were the captives.

The deer in particular were of concern to us. They tamed easily, and we didn't want to create animals dependent upon our small offerings of corn. One afternoon while Jeanne was cleaning up the garden, a doe that frequented the corn piles with a hearty appetite trotted down to the spot where Jeanne was working. The animal pawed the ground, made fleeting jumps in and out of the brush and finally stood her ground stomping. Jeanne went to the shed and filled a coffee can with corn. The doe followed and consumed the offering in a few minutes. Jeanne came into the cabin, and the doe followed once again. Jeanne went back outside, but did not feed the deer. We were trying to convince the deer that the corn was a treat, not the staple of their diet. Most of the herd came into the yard, ate some corn, and then browsed the dogwood. We planted clover near the driveway, and soon the herd was feeding nearby without depending on the corn. The birds also were given an allotment of sunflower seed, suet, and cracked corn. When it was gone, they sought their natural sources for insects and seeds.

By the end of October, the animals that would spend the winter with us were busily organizing their territories, readying their nests and making their presence known around the place. The noisiest of the crowd were the red squirrels. They spent frantic weeks trying to clear the yard of any intruder and even attacked the deer one late afternoon. Charging wildly into the herd, they succeeded in scattering the deer. But the deer returned. Once again the squirrels dashed beneath the many long legs, and hooves went sailing into the brush. On the third assault, the deer held their ground. Heads lowered, legs braced, the deer stared the squirrels into submission. Then all was quiet.

Jeanne and I went into the museum for the last time on the first of November. We insulated the windows and turned down the heat. While Jeanne attended to the packing of a Victorian clothing exhibit, I prepared the photographs for storage. Outside, a cold wind howled around the empty building. The lights in our office were turned low, and I caught one last look at the loggers who had lived here eighty years earlier. They were young and lean and ready to challenge the worst that nature could throw at them. They were ready for the long winter in the woods, ready for subzero temperatures and snow three feet deep. This land was a vast unsettled place, and they wanted to make it their home. They would cut the pine and clear the fields and break the hardpan with their plows.

I slipped each photograph into its envelope and dropped it into the file. Then I picked up a large picture made late in September 1894. As far as the eye could see were the remains of a forest, a farm, and the edge of what had once been a town. Everything was ash.

The wind had caught a loose board on the museum building and banged it furiously. When I got up to attend to it, I saw the Frank Haney story on the desk. I picked it up and slipped it into its place in the file. The land was ours now—for a time.

11

We woke abruptly to the crackle of gunfire and waited for our senses to catch up with the new reality of our once-quiet woodlot. There were many excited voices and shouts coming from the county road.

"Deer-hunting season," Jeanne moaned, pulling the quilt over her face.

"*Blot-Monat*," I said, leaning on an elbow and looking out the window over our bed. The sun had just risen.

"*Blot-what*?" Jeanne said, still buried deep in the covers.

"*Blot-Monat* means blood month. The Celtics slaughtered their cattle in November." I jumped out of bed and found my clothes. The evening grosbeaks had already gathered on the feeders and were chatting excitedly about all the commotion. Another volley of rifle fire echoed across the bog.

"Well, at least the Celts slaughtered animals for food. That's a lot more than you can say for some deer hunters," Jeanne said, buttoning her robe. She clenched a rubber band in her teeth and smoothed her hair back into a ponytail; all the while she paced from window to window in fierce hopes of finding a deer hunter on our property. There is probably no greater enemy of the deer hunter than Jeanne.

One year, while we were visiting the cabin on a weekend, Jeanne spotted several hunters hiking up our road. Our property is in a state game reserve, and we had posted it against trespassing. Nonetheless, the west side of the county road is open to hunting, and we often had hunters on our side, claiming to be disoriented.

"If you're disoriented, you shouldn't be carrying a gun," Jeanne said in her cool, five-foot-two voice. "If you aren't bright enough to read the No Hunting signs on the road, you shouldn't even be driving."

It was incredible to see three large middle-aged men in camouflage clothing and grease paint carrying .30-.30s, knives, and pistols hang their heads as Jeanne lectured them. When she had finished, she saw them to our gate and they walked to their four-wheel-drive vehicle and drove away.

I have not been so successful. When I have discovered a hunter on the place, the confrontation drags on forever. I do not share Jeanne's ability to see 'em, scare 'em, scold 'em, and scatter 'em. I end up having long discussions about the philosophy of land ownership or the good works of the National Rifle Association. My problem is that I get trapped by my belief in the right of the individual to bear arms. I see that right being exercised by hunters and I am proud of them, even though I'm disturbed that they are on my property. Jeanne believes in that right as well, but she believes further that the bearer of arms ought to be intelligent, and she does not find much intelligence in trespassers. We also worry about the arms bearers when we find bullet holes in our buildings, in road signs, and in our neighbors' cattle and dogs. Our No Hunting signs have been tom from their posts, four-wheel-drive tracks have appeared in the ditches, and beer cans have decorated the base camps of hunters along our road.

After a quick breakfast, we put on our jackets and hiked to a hill that overlooks the county road. Three dark vans were huddled together near our mailbox, and Jeeps and pick-ups were parked along the road as far as we could see. Sporadic rifle fire popped all around us. Jeanne took a deep breath and sighed. "Maybe the signs will do some good this year," she said. "It'd sure be nice to be able to work in the woods without getting shot."

A blue pick-up came down the road slowly. From the hill we could see rifle barrels sticking out of the open windows. Brakes screeched, and the truck stopped. Then it moved forward again slowly. "Hunting from their truck," I said.

"Yeah, real sportsmen," Jeanne said softly. "I'll bet they think they're big men today." The truck passed on, and we heard the brakes screech again. There was a tear on Jeanne's cheek.

"Let's go to work," I said. "I've got a lot of wood to bring in." We walked back to the cabin, and I gave Jeanne a tight hug. Hunting season was hard on her. Every day of the year we lived with a deer herd. We watched the deer grow from fawns to mature bucks and does. We watched them play, browse the dogwood, yard up in the winter, and follow the fresh spring trails to the bog in April. Jeanne tended the herd with care and appreciation for their need to remain wild. Yet she knew them, each of them, by a white patch here, a scar there, or by their weight or their eyes. They knew her, too. They would come closer to Jeanne than to me, they listened to Jeanne's soft voice but were afraid of mine. She talked to them, she reveled in the birth of each new fawn, and she defended them against the predations of man.

Jeanne also understood the "harvest." She knew and believed that the deer population, left unchecked, would grow and lead to disease that would maim and kill thousands of whitetails in a grisly death. She had no argument with the hunter who was skillful in his kill and hunted for food. But she hated the slob hunters who killed for the pleasure of using their guns, who so delighted in the chase that private property was overrun, and any animal of the woods was fair game for their fun. She hated the insensitive, the dullards, the hapless, and the bored who took to the woods during hunting season to prove they were alive. And at each sunset, when the guns fell silent, Jeanne watched the herd in her yard and breathed their names and crossed her fingers that none of them had been taken.

I walked back to my firewood deep in the forest. The axe I carried flashed in the sun, and my boots crunched through the leaves in the still, cold air. The rifles were silent for a time and as I worked the sounds of the forest returned. Death in the woods is not tragic. The crack of a rifle is but a momentary interruption to the tapping of the woodpecker. The thud of the striking bullet that fells the doe is but one of a thousand events in the passing moments of the forest. When the excited voices of men have died away, the chickadees sing and the blue jays scold and the woodpeckers tap their message on the rotted snag of the birch tree. And as the doe is dragged through the dried leaves and tied to the hood of a pick-up on the road, the fawn looks for his mother for a short time, then quickly finds cover, food, and the safety of the herd. The crows will call, the ruffed grouse will search for aspen buds, and the hare will feed on the bark of a fallen tree.

There is always death in the woods; it is death that gives life. And when the men have dressed their kill and cleaned their guns and parked their vans and opened their beer in front of a television set, the woods will live, the deer will feed in the moonlit pastures, the chickadees will call. The hunters will have conquered nothing.

I looked up to see Jeanne running down the trail. When she saw me, she waved. "Ted's here," she called. "He's here with the wood."

By the time we returned to the cabin, Ted had already started to unload the lumber. He looked angry and tired.

"I see you got company, too," he said, pulling out his Pall Malls.

"Company?"

"On the road. Hunters. We've got them crawling all over the road out there."

"Oh, them," I said, looking toward the road, happy not to see anything through the dense brush and trees, "Yeah, they've been around since sunrise, but so far we haven't had any of them up here. How about you?"

Ted lit a cigarette. "Yep. A couple of pick-ups came back to the new house and eyeballed it, but they left. Boy, signs don't mean nothing these days."

"I think they feel that any land outside the city is open to the public. When I tell them that we live here, they look shocked, like I'm trying to pull one over on them." I was eyeing the trailer-load of lumber that Ted had brought for our sauna project.

"Ted, that's a lot of wood."

"Well, you ought to be able to put up a sauna bath anyway, eh?" he smiled. "If there's wood left over, it'll make good kindling."

It took us a half-hour to unload the trailer of the long rough-cut aspen boards. Ted had thrown in enough studs and two-by-sixes to build a small house. "How much do I owe you?" I said, sweating in spite of the cold November wind.

"Nothing, I had to get the stuff off my place. Glad you can use it. I'll take a cup of coffee, though." A terrific volley of gunfire shattered the silence. "Sounds like they got a machine gun over there," Ted said as we walked toward the cabin. Ted and his sons were hunters, but they were skilled and careful and Louise canned the venison that they took every season. To Ted and his family, hunting deer was a way to stretch their food dollars; they wasted nothing.

Jeanne had coffee ready when we came into the cabin, and she'd made rolls, dripping with caramel, still steaming hot. We feasted in silence. Ted understood our attitude toward hunting. He had helped us understand the difference between shooting for fun and shooting for food. "I don't mind the real sportsmen," he had told us. "What I can't understand are the guys that think the season is the time to get out of the house and shoot up the countryside. Most of those guys can't tell the difference between a buck and a doe—some of them can't tell the difference between a deer and a steer."

When we finished our second cup of coffee, Ted told us what had happened on the road near his house. "I saw the pick-up driving real slow, and I went up to see what was going on. I knew what was happening— they were shooting from their truck. Well, they told me that they had seen a buck in my field and had taken a shot at him but missed. I told them that I didn't want to see them around here again, and they took off A little later I was out in the field, and I came on this doe that was shot up real bad. They had dropped her and then went over to see if it was a buck." Ted shook his head. "That's no way to hunt."

"Was it a blue pick-up?" Jeanne asked.

"Yeah, sort of pale blue," Ted said. "You seen them?"

I nodded. Jeanne filled the coffee cups. Outside, the evening grosbeaks flew from the feeders into the trees. A red squirrel sat up on a stump and looked around for the source of all the trouble. "We saw the truck on the road this morning," I said.

When Ted was gone, Jeanne and I measured the sauna site and I began to dig footings for the building. By sunset, after the rifles again thundered across the road, I was ready to lay the sauna floor. We ate quickly and waited for the deer to come to the corn. Long after it was dark we heard the familiar stamping in the yard. Jeanne went out to feed them, and as near as she could tell the herd was still intact.

The next morning the deer were in the yard early. They were nervous about the shooting across the road and equally curious. We watched while the yearling. Nosey, passed in front of the cabin and walked slowly up the hill that overlooked the road. There he stood for nearly an hour, watching the hunters, flicking his tail, twitching his ears, and browsing in the brush. He was having a tremendous time watching the hunters who were milling about on the road below.

"I think we're the only ones who worry about hunters," I said. "Nosey is a perfect name for that one."

"I just hope he stays in the refuge," Jeanne said. "Just for two more weeks."

"We can't hide here, Jeanne," I said, putting on my jacket. "We're going to have to take hunters and hunting along with everything else. It's going to happen every November, and there's nothing we can do about it. Two weeks out of a year isn't that bad."

"What about the poachers?"

"They're a part of this place, too. We aren't going to find it any better anywhere else."

"I know that," Jeanne said. "1 think about it when I'm with the deer. I tell myself that these few acres of ours are different, that it's a special place. Here the animals can be free and wild, and we can live in the middle of it all without having trophy hunters blasting it all away. But I know that isn't true. I know that you can't live anywhere in the bush and expect to find champions of wildlife preservation."

She dropped a piece of birch into the cookstove. "You know, I've been thinking about where we could go to live and get away from these weekend hunters."

"Where's that?" I said.

"Right back where we came from. Some cave of a home on the tenth floor of a condominium, where there's an *Audubon* magazine on the coffee table and checks made out to save the whales and the seals and the eagles. Remember?"

I smiled and watched the grosbeaks soaring back into the yard.

"Remember how we used to invite friends over for wine and cheese, and spend the whole night talking about our place in the woods? We looked at pictures and told stories and ended up having a long discussion about wildlife preservation. The city was the place to live if you wanted to appreciate wildlife and imagine a pristine wilderness out there somewhere. Our weekend forays to the bog didn't teach us much about the reality of nature, either. Remember the horror we felt when we saw the first rabbit get picked off by an owl?"

I looked out the west window and saw that several does had joined Nosey on the hill. Any one of the hunters on the road could have easily seen the deer if he'd been looking. "There's nothing like a crowd to attract deer," I said. "And I know what you're saying about viewing the wilderness from the city. I've felt it, too. That was the only place I've lived where I met anyone who really cared about preservation and fought for it with their congressmen. We know there are pockets of people around here who care, but they keep it to themselves. It isn't a popular attitude."

"No, I don't think I'd talk about it at the bar in the village," Jeanne laughed. "But what I'm trying to say is that having lived here for nearly a year now, I've begun to appreciate another kind of fullness about the woods and the bog and the animals that includes the humans as well. I think we're finally beginning to see the reality of the place and enjoying it for what it is."

Board by board, the sauna floor came together. The walls went up easily, and I was crawling around on what would become the roof when I felt I was being watched. I dropped the hammer and looked around.

There was nobody that I could see, so I went back to work. As I was lifting a piece of siding into place, I once again felt the curious presence of something just back in the woods. The walls were finished, the insulation was in place, and I had just started to climb to the roof when I noticed Jeanne waving at me to come in. I emptied my pockets of nails and started down the trail; Jeanne signaled me to come quietly. I looked around and saw nothing out of the ordinary. When I got to the cabin, Jeanne was excited. "Strawberry was here! Dick, he's an eight-point buck!"

We hadn't seen him for months, and I thought he was a goner. "Where did you see him?" I said.

"You'll never guess."

"No, I won't—where?"

"About ten feet from you on the trail, watching you build the sauna. I couldn't get your attention to let you know."

"So that's who was watching me. I had this feeling there was someone in the woods—I never thought it was a deer. Strawberry. He's back. Where is he now?"

"He went up the trail when you came in," Jeanne said. "But he didn't look like he was in any hurry to leave. I'll bet he comes back."

For the rest of the afternoon I worked on the sauna and kept an eye out for the buck. He was the first deer that we had managed to identify on the woodlot. He had a large scar on his flank that made it easy to spot him in the herd, and we soon discovered that he was an outsider, always chased away by the others. Then, the winter before we moved to the cabin, we saw Strawberry with an older doe who was also easy to identify since she had a metal tag in her ear. For some reason, Strawberry liked me. I would often see him in the woods watching me work. He was a spike buck the last time I had seen him up close. Finally, as I began to nail the sauna roof in place, I caught sight of him. I'd never seen anything so beautiful. He was strong and smooth with a thick coat of gray hair. The eight-point rack gave his head a massive appearance. He watched me for a moment and then turned his head toward the cabin. I returned to my work.

By late afternoon I was ready to install the sauna's sheet-metal woodstove. While Jeanne gathered water buckets, a thermometer, and wood for our first firing, I anchored the metal chimney and worked up a temporary door. We heaped rocks on the stove, nailed the window in place, and lit the fire.

The sun shone bright on the birch trees outside the sauna, and the smoke cast fleeting shadows as the temperature of the little room rose steadily. Jeanne and I perched on the high shelf and watched as the thermometer needle pointed to one-hundred degrees Fahrenheit.

"More wood," I said, shoving a couple pieces of birch into the stove.

We waited, peeling our jackets off and resting against the rough-sawn walls. One-hundred-and- twenty degrees; one-hundred-thirty, -forty, -fifty. We went out to cool off and collect wood.

"It's working," Jeanne said, smiling, with small beads of perspiration on her forehead. "Do you think we can take our first sauna tonight?"

"I don't see why not, but we had better get a pile of wood and let the place warm up for an hour or so."

The sun had set when we walked across the yard dressed in our robes and carrying pails of water. Jeanne had brought a couple of loofa sponges and soap. The temperature had risen to two-hundred-five degrees. We took off our robes and climbed up on the shelf; we began to sweat immediately. We watched the light fade in the forest through the small window, and soon all that we could see was the red-hot stovepipe and the faint orange color of our skin. We heard nothing through the heavily insulated walls, only the gentle ticking of the hot metal and the occasional crunch of a log settling in the fire. We said nothing; the tranquility of the sauna said it all. After a time, we left the room and stepped naked onto the deck under the stars and washed in cool water.

"Dick, listen," Jeanne said softly. There wasn't a sound to be heard. The weekend was over. The hunters had gone. The freeway south would be filled with their vehicles snaking slowly back to the city, the hunters' unshaven faces peering into the night looking for evidence of other kills. The hunters had their reward, and we had our quiet.

"After next weekend we won't see much of them until next year," I said, pouring a pan full of cold water down my back. "And in a few weeks we ought to be rolling in some snow when we take our sauna. Ready to go back in?"

An hour later we walked slowly through the night, ready for a deep sleep. The sauna had done its work—we had never felt so clean and fresh and willing to live our so-called primitive lifestyle. The simple life was rewarding beyond all expectations. We'd spent twenty dollars on a sauna that would have cost a thousand had we built it with a kit. Best of all, we had built it ourselves, we had shaped it to our needs with our own hands, on a piece of land that was ours once again.

12

There was ice fog on Thanksgiving morning, and we lingered in warm robes close to the woodstove. The radio reported snow north and south of us, but we looked out on a brown woodlot covered by only a light coat of ice. The deer came to the corn with frost on their backs, and, high above, several ruffed grouse perched in an aspen tree waiting their turn at the feeding stations. Red squirrels scampered through the yard chattering while blue jays and grosbeaks fed together in peace. A male hairy woodpecker flew out of the forest with loud clapping wings and landed on the suet bag where he tapped the frozen fat. Thanksgiving was in the air, and Thanksgiving was under the bed where Jeanne had stored the cranberries harvested from our bog after the first freeze in September.

"I think I'll cook the turkey for three hours," Jeanne said, looking over her woodstove notes. "I'm going to need a couple armloads of dry birch to keep the temperature up."

"I have a stack in the shed just waiting for this day," I said, lighting my pipe. As I looked at the fifteen-pound turkey on the counter, pink in the pale light, I thought how Jeanne had become a master cook using a woodstove these past nine months. I also remembered how her first pie had burned to a cinder. We had started a roaring blaze in the firebox of the cookstove and taken the oven's temperature. It was two-hundred degrees. We piled more sticks on the fire, but the temperature climbed to only two-hundred-fifty. Disappointed in the oven's heating ability, Jeanne put the pie in for a slow cook. In minutes, gray smoke filled the cabin. The crust of the pie was charred, the apples were raw, and the oven's temperature was well over eight-hundred degrees.

We had discovered the secret of the cookstove: It took time to heat cast iron, but when it got hot, it stayed hot, and any additional fuel pushed the temperature up rapidly. We found that it took an hour to prepare the stove for baking and that the temperature could be held constant by adding a single stick of dry birch every half-hour or so. It was a matter of feeling, and Jeanne soon developed the correct set of feelings. She learned to control excess heat by propping the oven door open with bits of matchsticks. There was one for three-hundred- and-fifty degrees, another for three-hundred, and others for cookies, roasts, and pies.

In nine months, Jeanne had so developed her abilities, and her bakery had produced such a bounty, that we each gained fifteen pounds of extra weight, most of it from pies. And now our Halloween pumpkin had been saved for Thanksgiving pie, and we found it in good shape under the bed with the cranberries. We discovered early in our stay that some parts of the cabin never warmed to room temperature and thus provided perfect storage for perishable foods. Fruits and vegetables were kept under either the bed or the desk, where the temperature was forty degrees. Dairy products survived winter and summer on the floor beneath the kitchen counter. Soft drinks and liquor stayed cool in the clothes closet with our boots. We had no refrigeration and no ice cubes until mid-November, so our visitors had to adjust to iceless cocktails.

So much of our lifestyle in the woods had evolved smoothly and with such convenience that we rarely discussed "improvements." Electricity was out of the question; we had found no need for it and no trouble living without it. Our life had become slow and even, like the breathing of a sleeping child. The lack of plumbing was neither a problem nor a challenge; it was simply a

fine way to live. Hand- pumping water to fill pails and kettles took
ten minutes a day, and hot water was always on the boil. The
outhouse, too, was a pleasure. There was so much peace in the
solitude of a morning toilet that we quickly forgot the mosquitoes
of summer and the wind-chilled updraft of winter. With the door
open wide, we watched the fog roll across the bog or followed a
flight of whistling swans at sunset. It was a quiet place to watch the
snow swirl and drift and to count the stars in the Big Dipper on a
cold, clear night. Many of the older people in the community
remembered the outhouse with a sigh and a faraway look in their
eyes. They smiled as we told about the deer resting not twenty feet
from the door. They nodded when we recalled the thunderstorm
that rattled the roof and shook the walls. They laughed when we
asked how to get the toilet seat warm when it was twenty degrees
below zero. "Take it in the house and hang it behind the stove, and
when you go out, don't waste no time," they advised us.

As I walked up the trail to the woodpile I looked back at the
cabin nestled in the brush still white with frost. I watched the
smoke from Jeanne's cookstove curl high into the cold air and out
over the bog. I always felt a little guilty when I saw the cabin from
a short distance. It seemed that it belonged to someone else. We
had been here such a short time and remembered so much about
our life in the city that we often thought ourselves visitors in a
wonderful place apart from the troubles of the outside world. What
right did we have to enjoy such comforts for so little money? What
we spent to live at the cabin for a month wouldn't have seen us
through three days in the city. And by what good fortune were we
here when so much of America had been forced to trim its budget
against inflation?

What we enjoyed knew no economic restraints. The changing
of the seasons, the call of the loon, the wind and the rain and the
snow that blew free— these were the things that we cared for, and
we knew they would not fall under the axe of partisan economic
theory. What gave us pleasure would not fail when federal funds
were withdrawn from state and local coffers. Important as

bureaucrats thought they were to the pursuit of safety and efficiency and effectiveness in lifestyle, they were useless to our well-being. Essential as power companies imagined themselves, they had been forgotten by us. We needed our neighbors, we needed the seed from last year's crops. We needed the water that flowed beneath our land and the heating fuel that was lying dead in the woods around us. From the earth we received our food, and from the earth we received our pleasure.

There was much to be thankful for on this Thanksgiving Day.

Blue jays called as I split dry birch deep in the woods. The sun broke through the fog, and the icy brush around me shined like cases of jewels at Tiffany's. If this was romanticism and sentimentality, if our philosophy of life had become simplistic, all I could want was more of the same. If we were missing something by living out of step, I prayed that we would never again hear the familiar drums. But when I looked above and saw the contrails of a large jet in the deep blue sky, I remembered that we were not living apart, that we were but two persons in a world of billions led by a few who would decide whether we lived or died in a Final World War.

The birch split easily in the cold air, the woodpeckers tapped their territorial messages on the hollow trunks of dead aspen, the sun cast long shadows and began its early descent in the southwestern sky. I loaded the wheelbarrow and started back toward the cabin. Whatever was to happen in the world, whatever mistakes would be made or solutions found, Jeanne and I would not forget these days. Our satisfactions, our happiness, and our love for each other were but seeds nurtured in this woodland place to grow stronger with time.

Even before I saw the cabin I could smell the turkey cooking, and when I came around the final hook in the trail, I saw the pumpkin pie cooling on the deck. Jeanne was pumping water, and the squeaky pump handle sang its song as loud as the evening grosbeaks perched in the tree tops. As the bright, clear water gushed from the spout, I felt again the sense of abundance in the earth. Jeanne, dressed in a bright red sweater, corduroys, and Sorel boots, appeared as natural to the setting as the icy birch trees that hung low over the cabin roof.

I recalled how she was as we prepared to go to work in the city: her camel-colored coat draped over a dining-room chair, her boots by the door, her voice singing as she combed her long black hair in front of the mirror in the hallway. I thought of the streets that we walked together in a sea of bobbing faces. I remembered the car horns and the sirens and the excited voices raised against a late-arriving bus. There were the phone calls that we made to each other during the day to plan a dinner or to discuss a party or just to hear the voice of the other. There were the trips to the airport and the kisses of goodbye and the long minutes watching the other disappear into the crowded terminal building. There were always the thoughts about the day that we would no longer be a part of that system, but be together for all time.

Jeanne carried pails of water into the cabin, and I pushed the wheelbarrow into the yard. There were others with dreams in the city streets. But we walked in ours alone, we walked in confidence that the day would come when the sounds of buses and airplanes and the crowds of booted feet would fade into the peeps and chirps of birds and squirrels. The smoke of engines would be caught up in a breeze, and the city would be gone. That day had come, and the dream had been true to its promise. The camel-colored coat lay deep in the trunk.

"Louise called," Jeanne said as she retrieved the pumpkin pie on the deck. "She's coming over for coffee in a few minutes, and she's bringing Buckwheat." Buckwheat was a six-month-old golden retriever who belonged to Ted and Louise's daughter. He was a fully charged puppy, a fifty-pound bundle of excitement that had often visited our place. Jeanne and I loved him. Both of us had always had a dog in our life, and we thought a great deal about finding one to join us at the cabin. What had stopped us was our concern for the wildlife on the place, especially the deer. We had come to the woods to watch nature, not to set up housekeeping with domestic animals in the center ring. Yet as we sat before the fire on a cold night we talked about the empty spot on the rug in front of us. The cabin looked as if a dog were missing.

When the pick-up truck drove into the clearing and the retriever shot out of the back to meet us, Jeanne and I looked at each other and sighed. "If we could find the *right* dog...."

"Hey, you two, I can smell your turkey all over the county," Louise said, carrying a package wrapped in tinfoil. She held it high to keep it from the jaws of the dog who obviously knew the makings of a party. Jeanne relieved Louise of her package, and they slipped into the house while I distracted Buckwheat with a stick. We played for a few moments and then started a hike up the trail. He stayed close as we walked, but jammed his nose into every hole we passed. His great feathered tail swished from side to side, and then he exploded out of one hole to look for another. On the ridge he caught the scent of the deer herd. He looked around, he looked at me, and then he was gone like a bullet. "No!" I yelled, and the dog dropped to the ground. He returned to me on his stomach and rolled over at my feet, flashing brown eyes and the best smile he could muster on short notice. "Good boy," I said, patting him and wanting for all the world to own him. We ran all the way back to the cabin.

"He can stay outside," Louise said, pushing the cookies she had brought to the center of the table. "He isn't much of a house dog."

"That's fine," Jeanne said, petting the big red dog who was beside himself with pleasure. "This is just a cabin, perfect for a dog —isn't it?" she said to the dog and me. I caught her eye as I filled my coffee cup. She smiled and shrugged her shoulders. I sat down on the couch and was joined there by Buckwheat, who fell asleep in my lap.

"In my house that dog would be in trouble," Louise said.

"It's fine, Louise," I said. "He's probably cleaner than I am."

We chatted for a while, and as I stroked the dog I saw in Jeanne's eyes a sadness that I hadn't seen there in some time. She stared at Buckwheat, and I could hear her wheels turning.

"Louise," Jeanne said suddenly. "If your daughter ever wants to give up that dog, you know where there's a home for him."

Louise looked at Jeanne for a moment and smiled. "Well, she really thinks a lot of Buckwheat, but I'll tell her. You really ought to think it over, though, before you get serious about a dog. You don't want to lose your wildlife, do you?"

"We think if we could find a bright dog, we could train him to stay away from the deer," Jeanne said. "But you're probably right. I suppose we'd lose the raccoon and the ermine and maybe the rabbits...."

"Well, have a good Thanksgiving and be sure to stop by tonight for a drink. I'd better get home and get our bird out of the oven. We have pie, too." She looked at the dog. "Come on, Bucko, your soft life is over." The dog stretched and followed Louise outside. As they drove away and it was again quiet in the yard, Jeanne and I walked into the woods.

"You'd think we could find a dog that didn't chase deer," she said, picking up a deep red maple leaf and dusting the ice off its sharp edges. "I bet Buckwheat is smart enough—if we worked with him."

"I think we're going to have to forget Buckwheat," I said. "Anyway, he picked up the deer scent on the ridge and took off like a shot. It would take a lot of work with any dog to keep it off the trails around this place."

"Louise is probably right," Jeanne said. "We should forget about having a dog. Still, he looked at home in the cabin."

Low clouds began to move in from the southwest, and radio reports warned of heavy snow. I filled the woodbox and built up the stack of birch on the deck. Jeanne announced that the turkey was ready to carve, and while she mashed the potatoes I sliced the bird into long, thin ribbons of steaming white meat, tasting Jeanne's good works frequently.

"Are you going to wait for dinner, or should I bring your plate to the counter?" she asked. "See if you can put the cranberries on the table without nibbling. I've got to go out and feed the deer."

I looked up and saw the herd filing into the clearing. The lead doe had her usual surprised-that- the-corn-isn't-out-yet look on her face. As I turned away from the window I thought that I had seen something else. I looked back toward the ridge and grabbed the binoculars. A second herd. There were at least a dozen deer coming down from the ridge. I tapped on the window as Jeanne walked by and pointed to the ridge. She nodded and in turn pointed to the south hill. A third herd. Jeanne poured several piles of corn and restocked the bird feeders, watched all the while by some thirty deer. When she returned to the cabin, I was wiping cranberries off the binoculars.

"Can you *believe* it?" she laughed, throwing her down-filled vest on the bed. "They're all coming for Thanksgiving!"

"I've seen a couple of them before, but look at all the fawns. I wonder where they've been all season."

"Maybe there's a snowstorm coming," Jeanne said. She was looking out the west window. "It's getting pretty dark over there."

Each group of deer moved cautiously into the clearing. Our regulars seemed baffled by the sudden increase in the population, and the old doe had her ears pinned back, challenging the outsiders to come near her corn. Fawns trotted all over the yard in mock attacks against each other, but the does quickly found and defended a pile of corn. Jeanne and I sat down to our first Thanksgiving dinner at the cabin.

Soon most of the deer were peacefully feeding. Every once in a while a doe would get too close to another, and they would rise on their hind legs and thrash at each other with sharp hooves. The birds, meanwhile, flocked to the feeders, and sunflower seed shells showered to the ground like snow.

"Some Thanksgiving, eh?" I said as Jeanne cut large pieces of pie. "We never dreamed that we'd have a deer herd feasting right outside our window. In fact, I can't remember what we thought we'd have a year ago."

"We were still trying to figure out how we were going to live here," Jeanne said, scooping whipped cream onto our pie. "I think we'd begun to believe that a move was a long way off."

A hare had joined the deer herd in the competition for the corn. He dashed from one pile to another, upsetting the older does who bobbed their heads and stamped their feet. Jeanne and I sat by the window watching the wildlife we had attracted. Our yard was like a great stage with many colorful actors coming in out of the wings. The grouse, always late, ran to the corn piles that were now dust and pecked the hard ground for leftovers. The rabbits circled, chasing each other. The deer wandered back into the forest one by one, and we counted only a half-dozen resting on a nearby hill. The clouds rushed by overhead, but there was no snow.

On December 1st the temperature was only twenty degrees above zero when we woke, and it fell all day. We cut wood during the morning and packed a lunch for a hike on the bog. The frozen mosses crunched beneath our feet, and the cold wind had given us rosy cheeks by the time we finally arrived in the spruce grove. We searched diligently until Jeanne found what we were looking for.

"Here! It's perfect," she said, rubbing her cheeks with a mitten. "It was born to be a Christmas tree."

The squat black spruce was about five feet tall and nearly as broad, and it was growing tight against several taller trees. I tied a long white cloth to its upper branches.

"We'll come out and get it in a week or so," I said as we snuggled down amid the dense spruce for lunch. "At least we'll know which tree it is if we get a lot of snow."

"I sure hope we get some soon," Jeanne said. "I bet the frost is down about six feet by now." The wind pushed hard against the evergreens, but we were quite warm in our wool sweaters seated deep within the grove. The clouds looked like snow, but it didn't come for another week.

On December 9th it snowed all day, and the temperature dropped the following day until it had reached twenty below zero. The wind seemed to pass straight through the cabin, and the Jotul stove worked hard to keep the inside temperature above fifty degrees.

Each morning we hustled into our sweaters and stocking caps as the room was slow to warm. After a hearty breakfast we took to the woods and cut firewood until noon, when we retreated to the cabin and found warmth in hot bowls of soup. The afternoons passed quickly as the days grew shorter, and we lit the kerosene lamps by four o'clock.

Never had we enjoyed ourselves as much as we did during those weeks before Christmas. Everything about our life in the winter had become brisk and bright and filled with simple chores that brought us in from the cold and together, warm by an evening fire. Never had we had so little money and so great a satisfaction. And when the frozen trees cracked like rifle shots in the night, when our windows iced over and the coyotes howled beneath the full moon on the first night of the winter solstice, we huddled in our warm quilt and lay awake for hours in the snowy wonderland.

We brought in our tree and decorated it with strings of popcorn. Jeanne hung our stockings on the mantle and filled them with nuts and candy. Green boughs decorated the shelves and the door, and the table was filled with plates of cookies. When Christmas Eve had come, we waited as expectantly as two children for the Yuletide Spirit to arrive. It had been a day of blue skies and grosbeaks, a day of many deer, rabbits, and squirrels. And when the darkness came and the faint kerosene light shone on our tree and the fire warmed our feet as the wine had warmed our hearts, the Spirit came into our home.

13

It occurred to me on Christmas morning that I had never known such a home as our cabin on the bog. The building was less substantial than garages we had owned, but its atmosphere was warm; the cabin was a comfortable place that seemed alive and as natural as the out-of-doors. There were no pipes snaking through its skeleton to interest plumbers; no wiring to attract electricians and government inspectors. It was a simple wooden structure that asked little attention of us, yet gave much shelter.

Jeanne and I had grown up drawing dream houses in our school notebooks. We had sketched vast rooms, great fireplaces, and big windows that overlooked hazy mountain ranges above crystalline lakes. It had not troubled us, in our youth, to consider that a house might not be a home. It was grandeur that we were after. As we grew older we each lived in a variety of places; some were charming, some were exotic, some were cold and acrylic atmospheres where our heartbeats were the only evidence of life. It was in such a place that I first drew this dream home, and what I drew was a small wooden box set deep in a bright birch forest. What I was looking for, I suppose, was a simple shack that would get me as close as possible to nature. I was thinking of Jeanne when I made my sketch; I was thinking about deer and grouse and bear. When we made the decision to move to the woods, we combined our ideas. Gone were the lofty windows, the microwave kitchen, the wall of electronic playthings, sunken tubs, and deep-pile carpeting. Our life, our home, would be dependent upon wood chips, not silicon. Our pleasures would come from the world outside, not from the household conveniences that made living a hardware-management problem. A home, we decided, was a place where we would be comfortable, where we would be together and in control of our life.

The Christmas tree filled our small room, and the presents glittered in the bright winter light. The woodstove hissed, and the coffee pot steamed while Handel's *Messiah* played on the radio. Jeanne had put the caramel rolls on a shelf to cool while we sat in front of the window and watched the deer at the corn. This day, our life on the bog was the Christmas present that we had given each other, and it was the greatest gift we had ever received.

The temperature was twenty degrees below zero when we woke and had breakfast. During the morning, clouds moved in and we dressed for a hike. The wind was light and the air was fresh as we stepped into the birch forest. The tracks of rabbits and squirrels crisscrossed each other and stopped at trees and piles of brush. The deer that had come earlier were gathered on the ridge, and we walked past them to the south following a new trail that would take us to a place we called "the popple forest." Here, the aspen trees were old and tall, and the forest floor was open. A raven croaked as he flew above the tree tops, and chickadees followed us as we pressed deeper into the woods. We were planning to open a new firewood cache on this part of the property, and as we walked I counted the trees that were dead and standing.

"If we're using a tree a week, I've already counted enough to get us through March," Jeanne said. "But I sure don't see how we're going to get a sled over all this fallen timber."

"We'll have to wait for more snow," I said. "There's enough fuel in here to keep us going for a couple of years if we had a foot of snow to skid it out." We stopped and rested for a moment, and a few flakes of snow began to fall. I looked at Jeanne and smiled.

"That's what I like about this place. You ask for snow and you get it."

"What's this thing?" Jeanne asked, pulling on a long, dark object that was sticking out from under a log. We brushed the snow away.

"It looks like a long crowbar," I said, inspecting the rusty iron rod. "Let's dig it out."

For some time we pawed at the earth with sharp rocks until the bar was free. It had a chisel point at one end and a hammered blunt surface at the other. "I think it's called a tunneling iron," I said. I measured the rod with my hand and decided it was about five feet long. "Loggers would have used it like a crowbar. Sort of an all-around handyman's tool. Isn't this where we found the metal straps?"

"I found some up the trail a ways. Do you think this was a lumber camp?"

"Not a camp, but someone was sure working in here. By the looks of this bar, it's been here a long time."

"During the fire?"

I looked around. The aspen growth was dense, and most of the trees I had cut were forty to fifty years old. "I'd bet that these are the tools of a pulping operation. They were probably in here in the twenties or thirties. This is really a different forest than the aspen up the trail."

"But it's low ground, and that would make a difference. In the spring we'd be sitting in a couple inches of water here," Jeanne said, scraping the iron bar with a rock. "Sometime we ought to spend a couple of days digging in here. I bet we'd run across a lot of logging material. We could probably put a whole exhibit together for the museum next year."

I placed the iron bar against a tree near the trail so we could find it when we returned, and then we walked on. I had a chill thinking about the people who had been on this land before us. Again I thought of the loggers camping beneath the white pine. There had been scores of hunters and pulpers who had made this place their home for a short time. And when they had gone, the bracken fern grew over their fire pits and the hazel covered their trails. Then it was wild again.

"You really don't own the land," I said quite suddenly. Jeanne looked at me and nodded. "I've heard that so many times, but it doesn't sink in until you've discovered artifacts."

"Or trails," Jeanne added. "It's when I see the remnant of an old trail that I get the feeling that the land isn't ours—it belongs to time."

The snow was falling faster now. We had found another log to sit on and listened to the woods. The sounds were subtle. Through the hissing of the dry snow we could hear a pair of hairy woodpeckers that lived near the popple forest. We heard a rabbit in the brush behind us. Chickadees were everywhere passing by in small explosions of flight; a few stopped on a nearby branch and studied us, gave a sharp dee-dee, and flew off into the snowstorm. We sat for a while longer and then started back toward the cabin. The snow stung our faces, and the brisk wind tugged at our collars as we worked at staying on the narrow trail. We picked up an armload of birch and stumbled down the path to the cabin. Jeanne stopped suddenly.

"Dick, redpolls." She pointed to the feeders. "Winter's really here." We stopped and counted only four of the finches with bright red caps. "The rest will show up—just wait."

"Look who's watching," I said, nodding my head in the direction of four deer that were only a few feet away from us in the brush. "I think they're ready for lunch."

The snow continued throughout the afternoon and early evening. Deer stayed in the yard, and grosbeaks joined the redpolls and chickadees and blue jays at the feeders. We found our books, and wrapped in snug blankets, we whiled the afternoon away lost in adventures of the South Pacific. I had just come to the foredeck of the schooner when I heard Jeanne calling me in the distance.

"Dick, wake up, we need a fire." I opened my eyes to see only a shadow in the dark room. I was curled up tight in the corner of the couch, and my book was on the floor. "We fell asleep," Jeanne said. "It's eight o'clock."

The temperature in the cabin had fallen to forty degrees, and our Christmas dinner was cold as stone in the oven. I stepped outside and found several additional inches of snow blowing around in a cold wind. The pump was frozen solid. We had neglected to dismantle it before our unplanned nap. I brought wood into the cabin, and while Jeanne started a fire I hauled out a pot of warm water to thaw the pump. Ice formed on the handle as fast as I melted it away, but I soon won the small battle and freed the cylinder and drained the water from the pipe. We didn't need to destroy our well on the second cold night of winter. When I returned to the cabin and brushed the snow from my moccasins, Jeanne lit the lamps and was feeding the hungry stove. The wind seemed to come straight through the walls, and the blowing snow rattled against the windows.

"Nice nap?" I asked.

"The best," Jeanne smiled. "I'd do it again if you wouldn't mind raw potatoes. I think the turkey is cooked, but it's a little cool right now. Why don't you pour the wine, and we'll wait an hour for dinner."

We sat by the window and turned the lamps low. We toasted the first snowstorm and Christmas and the deer and each other. The wind rattled the shutters and swirled the snow and howled in the chimney. We ate very late, very warm, and very happy.

In the morning the world outside had changed. The trails were gone, the path to the outhouse had disappeared, and our woodpiles were hiding deep in caves of fine sculptured snow. The sky was bright blue, and the birch rose from the snowdrifts like white candles on an angelfood cake. Our car was buried in a drift, and we smiled at the thought of being snowed in for the rest of the winter.

"It would be fine with me," I said. "We could always get a ride to town with Ted and Louise if we had to."

Jeanne looked at me and shrugged. "Well, we don't have to go anywhere for a week or so. Let's leave it and see what happens."

I picked up a sled and started off for the woodpiles in the forest. Jeanne was busy chatting with the birds while she filled their feeders. The deer were on the ridge. I felt a little odd leaving the car in a snowbank; it had always been our task, the day after a snowstorm, to dig the car out. As I walked I realized I heard only birds. There were no snowthrowers humming in neighbors' driveways, no children laughing, cars spinning, or plows clattering in the streets. There was absolute stillness broken every few minutes only by the flutter of wings or the tapping of woodpeckers.

I split a sled-load of birch and started back. As I passed the ridge I heard a new sound. It was a scrapping sound that was familiar, but I couldn't place it. Getting closer to the cabin, I stopped again and listened. It was quiet; then I heard the sound again. I left the sled and hiked down to the pond. When I saw it, I stopped. Through the dense stand of aspen trees I watched as Jeanne's stocking cap glided in and out of view. Her scarf and hair trailed behind her as she turned in graceful circles, spinning on skates on a small patch of ice. I moved closer, still hidden by the trees. Here was an elf at play on a bright snowy day—alone on the pond, deep in the forest, a small graceful figure dwarfed by the tall trees. Her skates scratched the ice and rose slowly as if she were in a dream. I walked quietly back to my woodpile.

On New Year's Eve we crawled into our warm bed before midnight and fell asleep with the peace that comes after working hard in the cold forest. We made no resolutions, no promises to live better; we only agreed that what we had found at the cabin was priceless and that we should never give it up for anything else.

There were temptations. It had been nearly a year since I had held a full-time job that required great concentration. I missed being a part of a team that created products. I missed the pressures and the routine. Jeanne, too, felt something missing in our rural life. She had always worked with great energy and purpose in the city. Here on the woodlot happiness demanded only that we take time, that we spend time; here the purpose of work was the work itself

Friends in the city had written of jobs that we might get if we returned. They painted pictures of financial security and green pastures in suburbia. On long, cold, gray days, warm by the fire, we often talked of the city. At Christmas we remembered the busy streets gay with people and bright with lights. We thought of a warm house heated by gas, we thought of water indoors and a bathtub. Even as the snow drifted down outside our sauna window and we basked in two- hundred-degree heat, we talked about a small restaurant where shrimp tempura was the specialty and where we'd spent many nights planning our life in the woods. Sometimes we were frightened by our talk; we stopped short and didn't mention the city to each other for days. Always we decided that our cabin life was a superior way to live. For Jeanne and me the isolation, the woods, the primitive lifestyle all meant more than the security, the involvement and the old-age benefits of a good job in the city. Yet we talked about the city, we recalled city places, and when we had a visitor from the city we grilled him for information and images.

"I think he probably thought we were in a cage," Jeanne said one night after a friend left to go back to town. "We made him give us a status report on every play, every movie, every bar.... It's funny because we didn't care that much about that stuff when we lived there."

"When we lived in the city, we always compared its virtues to the country's. Now we've been away long enough to have lost the meaning of the city."

"You mean the grass in the city is starting to look greener."

"Right. We've lived here long enough now to make a comparison. I don't think we could have before now." "Well, I think we should stay."

"Me, too. No question."

On New Year's Day we walked to Ted and Louise's house for dinner. As we hiked away from the cabin and as the voices of birds faded, the boglands seemed hostile and cold. There was yet mystery in the empty place, but the thinning snow and the barren forests seemed devoid of any life at all. This is what we had wanted: a rough land where we could be alone, a place unattractive to most people. Beyond our property there were hunting cabins set back in the trees, drifted in, forgotten. Deer crossed the road in front of us, and even they seemed lost in the bleak landscape. We talked about the city again. We tried to imagine what we would be doing if we lived there. A flight of evening grosbeaks passed overhead, and then the silence rushed in behind them. Our boots scuffed the frozen gravel on the road.

"It's probably cabin fever," I said. "It has to be. We wanted this life bad enough to give up everything we had."

"If I ask myself what I want more than anything else, I keep answering: the cabin, the bog, this," Jeanne said, pointing at the tamarack swamp. "But I feel guilty, I guess. I feel as if we ought to be *doing* something...like we've been on a long vacation and now we should be returning to a job."

"But we aren't, this is it," I said, kicking at a stone.

"You know what's so hard is that we don't need much money, we don't have any payments to make. The car's snowed in, the cabin's comfortable. We're as free as the birds to do whatever we want, and it's driving us crazy."

Jeanne was right, of course. In the city we had to sweat out payments, meet deadlines, work. There were people we had to see, places to go. We were so busy maintaining our life—and we believed it was all so important—that we never thought about what it would be like to live without the bustle. When we came up here on weekends, there was so much to do. Flowers to photograph, insects to read about, trails to cut. When we left on Sunday night we were tired, but also rejuvenated to do our city work. We were living then. "We were bright and bushy-tailed and excited about everything we did," Jeanne said.

"Because we had a dream."

"Exactly. And we found it. We've come to the pot at the end of the rainbow, and now the magic is gone. We have to find a purpose here."

"The museum?" I said.

"I think it has to be broader than the museum itself. We've become very interested in the history of this area, and you say you want to do some writing. Maybe we ought to write about this place —there are a lot of stories in here."

Ted and his son waved at us from their deck. The smell of woodsmoke was reassuring.

It stayed cold the first week of January, but when I came down the trail one morning I met Jeanne returning from the mailbox warm with excitement.

"The seed catalogs came!" she said. She hugged me and danced around, flashing the thick brochures decorated with photographs of brightly colored flowers We ran inside the cabin and filled our coffee cups and settled into our chairs. The pendulum on the clock over the mantle swung slow and easy as we read about the Big Boy tomatoes and imagined neat rows of peas, beans, and lettuce. Jeanne's eyes shone bright as she turned the pages filled with orange-red tiger lilies, butterfly glads, and fragrant freesias. We read aloud the aromatic names of springtime: Basketvee tomato, Ruby Queen beet, Butter King lettuce. Zippy peppers, and Edible pod peas. There were Gurney Girls and Walla Walla onions and No Burp bush cukes to bring summer into our winter afternoon.

I was putting wood into the stove when a letter on the table caught my eye. I opened it and handed the enclosed check to Jeanne.

"It's the children's magazine. They just bought our first story," I said.

Jeanne dropped the seed catalog in her lap. "I think I'm beginning to see our purpose here," she said. "Do you want to leave it now?"

"Not for the world," I said. "Not for anything in the world."

14

A small battery radio was our only access to news of the world, and we soon discovered that the nonvisual medium had sharpened our sensitivity to events around us. In the city, news magazines and television had provided for us images of a troubled world; words and pictures had so completely satisfied our curiosity that the real world seemed a mere sideshow that had found a niche in the universe of toothpaste and underarm deodorant. Our imagination slept as the big noise of the super-media stormed our consciousness with orange-faced reporters teasing victims of disaster to tears. We were voyeurs on safari with the Fourth Estate in the sorrier realms of human enterprise.

In the woods, tuned only to radio news, our visual senses roamed free to find balance; radio was a presentation of faceless fact that we weighed against the reality around us: the forest coming to life in the spring, birds gathering for migration, deer herding in the yard during a winter snow, the earth that gave us our food and water. Rather than feeling a diminished responsibility as citizens, we felt close, able and ready to empathize with our world neighbors. We were no longer mesmerized by the sheer weight of disaster, but finally able to see the humanity beneath the rubble of political misadventure. We felt as strong a kinship to the unemployed in Britain as we did to jobless steelworkers in America.

The plight of Japanese fishermen aboard a foundering vessel in the North Pacific gripped us firmly as we worked in the woods. Snow was falling, and visibility on the bog was reduced to a few hundred feet. We thought of the ocean and the small boat bobbing and the aircraft searching the enormous gray sea. I listened for the cries of men in lifeboats and for the thunder of the rescue planes that I half expected to fly low over our own birch island.

We had gained freedom from information. We had gained control of the switch that admitted the racket of the newsmakers, news reporters, and their commercial sponsors into our lives. It may have been an unrealistic tack in a time when the world seemed so small and its troubles so great, but we learned that better than being informed through the analysis of others was being in control of ourselves. We knew who we were, what we were doing, and why we were doing it at a time when disorder had disturbed the gyros of American leadership and many of our countrymen had lost sight of their dream. We were simply in a position to view our course clearly by having stepped out of the media events and onto a quiet hill where we could see beyond the chaos.

On January 20th we came into the cabin often and drank hot coffee while the snow melted on our boots. Our government was in transition, and the American hostages held in Iran were to be returned to their homeland. There was heavy fog at ten in the morning and the evening grosbeaks came to the feeders with ice on their breast feathers. Deer gathered in our yard as President Carter and Ronald Reagan left the White House together to attend the inauguration ceremonies at the Capitol.

CBS Radio reported that the American hostages were at the Teheran airport preparing for their flight to Algeria. Red squirrels buried seeds, and the radio played *Born Free*. A newsbreak at 10:26 reported that the hostages had departed Iran. WCCO's Joyce Lamont gave a recipe for All Season Apple Jelly, and Carter and

Reagan arrived on the inauguration platform. Redpolls landed on the feeders frightening the grosbeaks, Jeanne dressed to hike down to the mailbox, and at 10:33 we heard that there was some confusion: the hostages were still in Iran. The deer lifted their heads to watch Jeanne as she walked down our road. "Nancy Reagan has arrived on the platform, and her red dress fairly gleams in a crowd of somber people," CBS reported.

A hush fell over the inaugural crowd as George Bush was introduced. The grosbeaks returned to their feeders; the deer moved to the hill south of the yard. A flight of chickadees landed in the trees as Jeanne brought the mail into the cabin and stamped her feet on the rug by the door. Ronald Wilson Reagan was introduced amid a trumpet fanfare and shook hands with Bush. Two grosbeaks swung easily on a feeder. It was 10:45 on our clock.

Sources said the hostages were free, CBS reported, but Iran denied it.The deer were coming to the window.

Justice Potter Stewart administered the oath of office to George Bush, and Jeanne handed me a seed catalog from the morning mail. "God bless you, George," Stewart said. The Marine Band played *God of Our Fathers*, and I read that Super VFN Hybrid tomatoes were resistant to root knot nematodes.

Chief Justice Warren Burger was now swearing in the new president. The red squirrels chased the blue jays, and Jeanne went out again to give the deer more corn. "Preserve, protect, defend...." At 10:52, there was a twenty-one-gun salute, and after everyone on the inauguration platform shook hands, the new president began his speech. "The federal government did not create the states; the states created the federal government," Reagan said.

At 11:24, the band played *Hail to the Chief*. It was fifty-five degrees and partly cloudy in Washington. It was twenty degrees and foggy in the yard where the deer were eating the corn. It was dark in Iran. It will be raining in Algeria when the hostages arrive. I went out and brought back an armload of firewood while Jeanne made lunch. We had tomato soup while the radio played America. Bells were ringing in Minneapolis, and there was a large yellow ribbon tied around the Foshay Tower; a reporter on the street said there were smiles on the faces of everyone. "Tie a yellow ribbon 'round the old oak tree...."

When we came in from our evening hike, the hostages had arrived in Algeria. It was eight o'clock, and we had a full moon. The shadows in the forest were strong, the moonlight was bright. The news people were speculating about who had gotten off the plane and who hadn't. We thanked God that our people were safe, and then we turned off the radio. Deer moved in the yard from shadow to shadow. Coyotes yipped from the bog.

The January thaw brought warm temperatures to the woodlot and red squirrels to the deck to eat peanuts from our fingers. We dressed in summer shirts as the forty-degree winds buffeted the alder and hazel and melted the banks of snow. The trails became wet, and our wood-gathering was slowed as the sleds refused to move in the mud of the deep forest. We sat in deck chairs and leaned back against the south wall of the cabin and let the sun soak away our morning chills. Time slowed as the days grew longer, and although an arctic air mass was poised a hundred miles to the north, we could feel the coming of spring. The winds carried the smell, the snow rotted, and leaf buds expanded— ready to explode in May. Spring comes the slowest of all seasons, and the surest.

Then the snow began to fall and excited weather reporters forecasted extreme cold to follow the storm. We brought wood into the cabin and stacked it by the stove to dry. It is usual for those who heat with wood to get up a year's firewood in advance of the winter, and we naively thought we had. But each day, when I hiked back into the forest to draw from our savings account of birch, I noted the rapid decline of our reserve. The January thaw had fooled us into complacency and now with snow on the wind and arctic air rushing in on the coattails of the storm, I prepared the chain saw for the tough job of trying to catch up with Mother Nature.

As fast as I could cut the dead, dry trees, however, the woodstoves made ash of them. Each morning I rose, washed my face in freezing water, gulped down coffee and an egg, and tramped out into the woodlot. By noon I had toted several sled-loads of aspen and birch to the deck, yet at sunrise the following day we were in need of more.

The principal reason for the rapid consumption was the wood itself. Dead wood is often rotted by moisture and the work of insects. In the country they call it "punky" wood. When a tree falls to the ground, it is instantly claimed as home by ants and beetles and wasps. The insects dig tunnels and cavities in the heart of the wood, and that permits moisture to collect and break down the fibers of the tree. Standing dead wood is often in better shape, but many of these have been taken by woodpeckers and other birds for nesting sites. We always checked standing timber, dead or alive, for evidence of nests before we cut them.

Sometimes we found a prize aspen that had fallen and been debarked by rabbits and deer. The wood would be dry and solid, giving us quick heat. Dead birch trees tend to "punk out" in a single season. The bark is strong and resistant to moisture, but this protective covering serves to accelerate the rotting process inside. It is not uncommon to find a tall standing birch that is little more than bark holding up a column of dusty wood. Such birch bark was valuable to us as a fire starter, but the tree that it had protected was useless.

When the storm had passed, the cold air moved in as promised. We woke to a cabin temperature of thirty degrees. By noon we had raised the temperature to fifty, but a strong northwest wind often offset our efforts and we spent much of the day firing the stove as though it were a locomotive in a race. Our hands were cold, our feet were cold, and we wore sweaters and hats all day. In the cabin diary we underlined a commandment to ourselves: Get wood up early.

Days passed when Jeanne and I would see little of each other. After breakfast she gathered her saw and sled and headed out to the south, while I pulled my sled north. It was a bright day when one of us would find a solid, dry aspen to bring home. The work was pleasant. Dressed in wool pants and sweaters, we worked happily in temperatures of twenty below zero. When there was a wind, we wore face masks and a light windbreaker, but working in the woods was a far different matter than hiking in the woods. Our greatest concern was getting too warm and sweating while we chopped wood and then becoming chilled during the long hike back to the cabin. We never wore heavy jackets, which were simply too warm for the work we had to do. Both of us wore wool underwear, wool socks, and wool pants. Under the sweaters that Jeanne had made we wore light-weight shirts. Stocking caps, mittens, and Sorel boots with fresh felt liners completed our outfit. More often than not, we abandoned our sweaters while we worked, and many times I found I was most comfortable giving up both sweater and shirt when the temperature got above twenty degrees below zero.

On many cold days in February we sat on the deck in the sun, in our long underwear, drinking hot coffee and watching the birds at the feeders. After work each day and before the sun set, we dressed in robes and slippers and hiked to the sauna. The deep heat worked our sore muscles limber, and what sweat we had left rolled to the floor in rivers. Steaming, we stepped into a snow bank in front of the sauna and basked in the cool drift until we once again returned to the hot bath.

"If we ever get caught up with our firewood, I'm going to miss this feeling," Jeanne said one afternoon in the sauna. "I can't remember anything that felt as good as a sauna after a hard day's work."

"I doubt that we'll ever get caught up," I panted, coming in from a roll in the snow. "But if we do, we ought to stay out there cutting for next year. I would've never believed that we would use so much firewood."

"Just now I'm grateful that we had this trouble during an easy winter. We could have had this lesson during a blizzard."

The following week was even colder. We had gathered enough wood to see us through, and our work in the forest was now directed toward the following winter. We began to think of twenty below zero as normal. When the temperature rose to ten above zero, we felt like children in springtime. We hiked, we birdwatched, we tracked deer and coyote on the bog. On cold, clear nights we watched the constellations and listened to the rifle fire of sap and moisture freezing in the trees. The deer joined us at night, they followed us as we walked the trails and crossed the frozen hummocks of the bog. In bright moonlight we hiked in a world so bright we could have consulted a map without a flashlight.

The very best of winter was upon us, and we drank it in. This was the season that we had come to the woods to experience. There were few people, no strangers, and our isolation let us reach deep into our minds for answers hidden by the chaos of fighting winter in the city. If we had ever wondered who we were and where we were going in our life, this was the place to ask the questions. This was the quiet that many people search for in long trips to the mountains and on exotic islands in the South Seas. Here was food and shelter and warm clothes— and love. We thought often of world disorder, of pain and hunger and the loss of spirit. It seemed impossible, on a cold night on the bog, that there could be anything but joy in a world so still, so sleepy in a warm winter wrap.

As we read our books before an evening fire we paused often to consider our good fortune. And when we pulled the quilt to our chins when the winds howled and the snows blew against our windows, we gave our thanks for having so little in a world where there was demand for so much. We had come to the bog to try our wits, to test our strength against the will of nature, and we had found that there was no test at all. There was work, but it required no great strength. One had to be careful, but far less careful than crossing a busy city street. Living simply was difficult only when we made it so, and our mistakes usually told us that we were complicating what should have been an easy task.

Our greatest mistake came as a surprise on a cold night while we huddled near the stove. The phone rang, and Jeanne had an abbreviated conversation with Louise. When she hung up, she returned to her chair looking troubled.

"What did Louise want?" I asked, my eyes on my adventure book.

"She wanted us to come over for a drink," Jeanne said. "I told her we couldn't leave the woodstove, and she seemed very put out."

"We haven't seen them for several weeks. Maybe they think we're becoming hermits," I said. I put my book down. Some of Ted's suggestions began to make sense. He had told me we ought to put an oil burner in the cabin so the place would stay warm while we were away. I hadn't understood what he meant at the time, and I told him we were planning to stay tucked in at the cabin. Since the arrival of the cold weather, we had turned down numerous invitations to go visiting. Our stoves, unattended, would hold heat for several hours, but not long enough to combat the chilling winds that robbed the cabin of its warmth. When we had made necessary trips into town and had been gone for four hours, we returned to find the cabin temperature in the thirties on a day when the wind chill was twenty below zero. Starting a new fire to warm the place up took a lot of valuable wood. To leave the cabin after dark meant shutting down stoves, blowing out kerosene lights, and pushing a tubful of hot ashes under the engine of the car to get it started. It was plainly easier not to go anywhere during the cold months, and that's what we had planned.

The social fabric of the country, however, is a cloth of tight weave. Everyone on the road counted for something, and when problems occurred—if there was sickness, a fire, or a building to put up— each member of the community was expected to pitch in. We had been on the receiving end of this generosity many times, but had seldom returned the favor. Visiting was an obligation, a mandatory ritual, to assure the participants of cohesion in the group and solidarity of opinion and interest in the community. For many months we had been excused from our responsibilities, but

151

now, after nearly a year, we were being asked to show our hand, to put our cards down on the table where everyone could see them.

Louise had arranged our coming-out party without telling us, and one night, when we arrived at her home expecting to have a drink and instead met twenty of our neighbors in a game of whist, we realized how badly we had neglected our social duties. We were meeting for the first time people who lived within five and ten miles of us, and in the country those are next-door neighbors. The people were hard-working farmers and craftsmen who had deep roots in east-central Minnesota. They were from Swedish, Danish, German, Norwegian, and Irish families who had settled these boggy lands early in the twentieth century. The bond among these neighbors was strong, and Jeanne and I liked them all very much. But we still felt the need to hold on to our isolation, our basic independence.

We had hoped that over time folks would understand what we had come to the woods to accomplish. We wanted them to know that we were searching for a place where we could be alone with nature, where we could sit quietly and watch and not break the spell of the woodlot. We couldn't figure out how to tell our neighbors that if we had wanted electricity and plumbing, two cars, and an asphalt driveway, we would have stayed in the city. We had come to the woods to live in a cabin, to live simply, and if that lifestyle was offensive to the community, we would sell the land and move on. As it happened, we were afraid of hurting the feelings of people who turned out to be far more understanding than we were, and who had known all along what we were about.

We were still concerned as February passed, and when we turned down Louise's invitation that cold night, we decided to retreat for a few days to Minneapolis. We had errands to do for the museum, and we were curious about how we would feel back in the city after being gone for a year.

The night before we left, we took a sauna and lay for a long time under the bright stars. The temperature had risen to twenty above zero, and the snow felt warm on our heated skin. We talked and laughed about our trip the next day.

"I'm going to take showers, one right after the other," I said, rubbing snow on my arms. "Do you realize that we haven't had a shower for a year?"

"It's a bath for me," Jeanne said, looking up at the sky. "Water up to my neck, bubble bath, soft towels, and stereo."

"Stereo?"

"Records...maybe they don't call it 'stereo' anymore."

"I wonder if we'll really see a change in anything. A year isn't a very long time to be away."

"It *seems* like a long time," Jeanne said. "But if anything has changed, it's probably us."

In the morning we packed the van with everything that would freeze in the cabin. We drained the well and our water cooler, and put food out for the deer and the birds. I pulled the shutters over the windows, and we drove quietly to the village. While Jeanne arranged to have our mail held at the post office, I filled the van with gas.

"You guys got cabin fever out there?" the attendant asked.

"Something like that," I said. "We'll be back in a few days."

The attendant smiled and rubbed at a small spot on the windshield. "Yeah, it's nice to get out of the country for a little while—see the city again," he said. "A fellow can go nuts out here in the winter."

I picked up Jeanne, and we drove to the freeway. There was very little traffic. When the village was out of sight, Jeanne laughed.

"What's up?" I said.

"Oh, I was just thinking about what the postmaster said to me."

"What?"

"He said we probably had a case of cabin fever."

"Maybe that's all it is," I said.

15

We were nearly alone on the road south, but soon the city came out to meet us. Farm buildings had collapsed and large new signs in trendy colors rose from the wreckage announcing the development of future housing. *Peaceful Acres. Quiet Woods.* Everywhere the city was moving north, full of promises for the good life. In the nakedness of March, rows of colorful houses followed a small creek through an oak woodlot. Hooked together by asphalt roadways and manicured lengths of sod, the boxy houses faced the freeway and a mountain of landscaped cloverleaf that twisted the strings of traffic high above the rooftops of the settlement.

Trailer courts flicked past; industrial plants squatted in fields of gray snow, their parking lots filled with cars neatly spaced beneath huge electrical transmission lines. Then the city skyline was ahead of us. Bright in its gown of haze, it had grown some during the past year, and we were soon confused in the canyons of steel and glass. We felt alone and frightened as traffic passed us on both sides in a blur.

Jeanne's parents were to be gone for a few days, and we had been invited to use their house during our stay. We found the keys and dragged our pack sacks into a room with deep-pile blue carpeting, walls aglitter with gold-framed prints and French Provincial dressing tables. We stood a moment in our stocking feet inspecting our rough-hewn images in floor-length mirrors.

"I can't believe that's me," Jeanne said, turning in front of the glass.

"It might help if you took off your parka," I said. "But I have the feeling that the shaving mirror at the cabin kept a few secrets from us."

We prowled around the spacious house, trying the lights and the faucets and fiddling with the thermostat. When the furnace kicked in, we listened to the rush of warm air that filled the room.

"No wood to split. Just a switch. Not bad," I said, warming my hands.

"Not bad if you don't have to pay for it," Jeanne said. "Why don't you go ahead and take a shower. I'll wait for a nice long bath after we eat."

I didn't argue. I peeled off my clothes and was standing under the powerful stream of hot water in minutes. The sensation of water beating down on my back after a year of mopping myself with a sponge was fantastic. I used the shampoo and for the first time in many months managed to rinse my hair thoroughly. There were certain advantages to showers, I thought as I dried myself and put on clean clothes.

Jeanne, meanwhile, had discovered the FM radio and was searching the band for a stereo station. The sound was crisp and loud with character. Our little battery-operated radio at the cabin sounded like a toy by comparison. We settled back on a long white davenport, sipped gin and tonic, and listened. Outside, commuters were returning home and driving their cars into garages equipped with electric doors. Overhead a DC-10 whistled by in its approach to the airport. Light snow began to fall, and we sat close in perfect contentment with ice tinkling in our glasses and music in our ears.

The cabin, the woodlot, and the bog seemed a long way off; deep in an unsettled place, a rough place. We thought about the chickadees in flight to the feeders and the deer standing on the trail watching the cabin for signs of life. The living room darkened; the tiny lights on the stereo panel projected their amber rays across the coffee table where our empty glasses caught the color and held it fast against the night. More jets hissed overhead, and cars with headlights piercing the blowing snow moved across the picture window like tropical fish in an aquarium. Jeanne reached over and turned on a light.

"We don't have to sit in the dark and watch cars," she laughed. "I think I was really waiting for a deer to show up."

"Me, too. It must be time for the news. Want to see what Reagan looks like in the flesh?"

"TV? I'd forgotten. It's in the basement. I'll bring some hamburgers down in a minute." Jeanne checked the light as if it were a kerosene lamp.

I turned on the set and watched old familiar faces introduce a catalog of world problems. The reporters wore grim expressions and looked a bit older than I remembered them. I twisted the knob and watched another channel, which looked the same as the first. Everyone in the news business seemed to have a helicopter, and noise from the rotor blades served as background to an excited reporter's voice. The serenity of the suburb was not evident in the local news program reporting fires and bank robberies.

Later, while Jeanne was singing in the bathtub, I settled into a deep, soft chair in the darkened living room and listened to the radio. If we ever return to the city to live, I'll spend my nights like this, I told myself I'll hide from the television and from the neighborhood and from the bright lights of downtown. I'll grip the arms of a soft chair and wait for the sun to rise.

The next morning we woke to the buzzing of the clock-radio, and after passing the machine back and forth for a while, we finally figured out how to turn it off. The sun was rising, and electric garage doors were opening, and a flock of commuters were heading out into the quiet streets.

"I wonder what they do at night," Jeanne said, watching them.

"Probably the same thing we did," I said. "Is that the toast burning?" Jeanne ran into the kitchen.

As we finished breakfast we watched the second shift of "workers" leave their homes. Wrapped in quilted snowsuits and moonboots, an army of little scholars marched to the bus stop, where books and bags were stacked and a snowball fight was organized. "Miss the city yet?" I said.

"Not yet," Jeanne smiled. "But there's a lot going on down here. I feel like we ought to be doing something and not just snooping by the window."

We dressed and listened to the traffic reporter call out the progress of commuters entering the city. "Highway 12 is backed up...an accident is being cleared away. And 35 southbound is slow going this morning...." The daytime talk shows were promising experts who would discuss women's rights and abortion.

We backed the Volkswagen down the driveway and took the side streets into the core of the city. The errands we had to accomplish were simple, and we quickly found a spot in a parking lot. All about us people were rushing to their offices, stepping carefully around ridges of slush.

"Remember this?" Jeanne said. She pointed to the corner where we'd said goodbye to each other so often. "There's my bus!"

We watched the passengers climb aboard, and caught the pungent diesel odor as the large red bus pulled into the stream of traffic. Jeanne pulled me toward a coffee shop.

"I really do miss something here," I said, hanging my vest on a chair. "The electricity, the energy... there's something happening here. Everyone has some place to go."

"You know that isn't true," Jeanne said. "There's as much apathy here as there is in the country. You just don't find it downtown at 8:30 in the morning."

"Do you miss any of this?" I said.

"Sometimes, but I don't know exactly what it is. I think there's a certain security in schedules and defined duties. But I don't think I could live with that, and I don't think you could either, not anymore."

We walked with the morning crowds through city streets and finished our errands. I watched Jeanne at a counter where she was waiting for a salesperson. She was wearing her down-filled vest over a sweater that had a few threads of yarn torn loose. I remembered when she bashed through the hazel brush and caught that sweater on a branch. A woman nearby was wearing shoes with enormous heels. Her hair had recently been flipped into a kind of beehive that appeared to require a great deal of hair spray and a general avoidance of windy places. Her fingernails were long and bright red and matched her lipstick, and she carried herself with the care and concern of a bomb-squad member toting a dangerous explosive. When Jeanne was finished at the counter, she returned to me laughing.

"You sure have to show a lot of identification when you try to write a check dressed like I am," she said. "The saleslady kept looking at my Sorels and raising her eyebrows."

"I suppose we should have brought suits with us," I said. "At least you could have worn shoes with eight-inch heels."

"And I would have had to paint my toenails red."

Before we returned to Jeanne's parents' house, we drove over to the university campus where we had once spent much time in the natural history museum. It was there that we had studied the animals and birds that we had seen on the woodlot during our weekend visits to the bog. We walked again in a fast-moving crowd. This time it was students. They chattered and chirped like happy squirrels who had found the trail to a cache of sunflower seeds. There was confidence in their step and excitement in their voices, and it was a pleasure to hike in their company.

We entered the museum as if it were a temple of our new-found religion and strolled the corridors with an easy pace. So often we had left our offices and met in these halls. We had learned to identify the birds here; we had learned something of their environment and behavior. It was in here that we had met our squirrels and black bear and owls and hawks. Yet today the specimens looked very dead. The live animals we had come to know on the woodlot had replaced the models, and although the exhibits were still instructive, we felt homesick and decided to return to the bogland at once.

"We've done our shopping, let's go back home today," Jeanne said as we stepped out into bright sunlight. "I don't have any doubts anymore. I know where I belong. How about you?"

"I don't think I've learned anything new about the city," I said. "I'd rather live at the cabin, but...."

"But what?"

"I still feel like I'm missing something by being away from here. Maybe it's just the security you were talking about. In the country I feel isolated, apart, doing something that's not very important. I mean, who cares besides us that a black bear is prowling around outside the window?"

"I think that's the best part of our life in the woods," Jeanne said. "We enjoy the black bear, and we don't have to justify our pleasure to anyone."

"I agree, but I just sense a need for a purpose up there. There has to be a reason for us to continue to live apart from the system. My reason is to live with you, to be together surrounded by nature. I want to ski back to our wood piles and sit close together in our little shack during a snowstorm. But is that enough?"

"It's enough for me," Jeanne said. We stopped to look in a bookstore window. "I don't think we can feel guilty about wanting to be different," she said. "Our purpose is simple: We're living together in the woods, apart from the system, close to nature, because it's there we feel whole. Look at the books in this window. Half of them are about getting your life together. I don't think very many people feel complete. Since we moved to the bog I've felt complete. I think that's important."

We packed the van and made it to the freeway just in time for rush hour. Long lines of cars snaked through the northern suburbs while a local television station helicopter hovered overhead. The evening pageant of the roadways was being watched by thousands hugging their television sets while dinners cooked in their ovens. "The deer will be coming to the corn about now," Jeanne said. "I'd sure rather be watching them than a long line of cars."

"It won't be long now," I said.

We rode with the convoy for many miles north of the city, then one by one the cars turned off the freeway and headed for a suburb. Finally, we were nearly alone on the road, and the sun dropped below the horizon. The engine of the Volkswagen droned on as we watched the pink glow of sunset turn gray and then disappear in the black of night. I looked at Jeanne. Her lips were pressed together and her eyes shone bright; she had already arrived at the cabin.

Deer met us on the driveway and stepped aside as the Volkswagen crawled through the mud. The headlights bounced and flashed on the birch trees. A rabbit darted in front of us and zig-zagged ahead of the car up the sloppy road. We looked at the cabin a moment before I shut off the headlights.

"We're home," Jeanne said as the rumble of the road noise passed away and the quiet of the woodlot rushed in.

We unloaded the van in the dark and stumbled up to the deck of the cabin. I found the keys and tried to locate the lock in the dark.

"There's something hanging on the doorknob," I said, handing Jeanne a plastic bag of some kind. We pushed our way into the cabin, and Jeanne lit a kerosene lamp. The room glowed warm in the yellow light as I opened the stove door to lay a fire.

"My God!" Jeanne said. "Look at this!" She held up the plastic bag that had been hanging on our front door. "The Avon Lady has been here!"

I put sticks in the firebox and touched a match to a piece of birch bark; when the fire started, I shut the door. I looked at the plastic bag and at our reflection in the cabin window. The simple wooden walls; the cold, damp air; groceries stacked on crude open shelves—somehow it didn't add up to a visit from the Avon Lady. I pictured her struggling up the muddy driveway and staring at the cabin. She must have looked for the doorbell as she clambered up on the deck. There is none.

I opened the cabin diary and made a note:

We have just returned from the city. Found nothing there to our liking and left two days early to return to our wilderness home. Glad to be back with the deer and the bears and the birds—and the Avon Lady.

In the morning the sun woke us early, and we jumped into our clothes for a walk in the woods before breakfast. The temperature had risen overnight, and the melting snow had created a lake around the cabin. "This is where we came in," Jeanne said as we slopped across the muddy yard to the trail. "Today is the anniversary of our first year in the woods."

"You're right! We have to think of something to do, we have to celebrate!"

"Let's start by taking the hike. Dick, I never want to leave the woods again. Never."

"I don't either. I thought I might find something in the city, a sign or a feeling that we ought to go back. But all I thought about was this."

We walked slowly, very slowly, taking in every sound, feeling the branches that would soon sprout a fresh green leaf. In the pools of melted snow we saw our reflection and the backdrop of tall white birch against the March sky. In a week, the spring solstice would come, and every place on the earth would receive equal sunshine and darkness. The cold would retreat and the warm breezes would dry the mud, and Jeanne would be on her knees in the garden with a red bandana on her head. The deer would lose their gray coats and become a brighter brown. And then the red-wing blackbirds would sing from the road, and the purple finch would bathe in the shallows of the pond. We sat on a log on the ridge.

"You've found a purpose then?" Jeanne asked.

"Just to live simply and let all this become a part of us," I said. "Maybe just living well is purpose enough." When we returned to the cabin, the phone was ringing. Jeanne answered. "Louise! We got back late last night. No, we don't have any plans for lunch." She looked at me and smiled. "Fine, we'll leave right away." Jeanne put back the receiver and said, "I think they're planning a surprise for us."

"We've been here a year, I'll bet that's it."

As we drove up the road we saw the kids in the yard playing with the golden retriever. "Buckwheat's sure getting big," I said.

"He's almost a year old, he should be about grown. He's really beautiful."

Ted and Louise came out to our car to meet us, smiling. "Happy first anniversary!" Louise shouted. Ted and I walked around their house inspecting the melting snow banks while Jeanne and Louise went inside. It was good to be back with these friends who had done so much to make our first year a success.

I looked at Ted, who had long ago left his father's farm to find a future in the city, but had later returned. He had come back to the land, the rough land of east-central Minnesota, to raise a family and work the clay for his food. There was much in this man and his wife that Jeanne and I did not know. What we did know was that their love for each other and their family had been purpose enough to remain on this empty, brushy land.

When we finished eating lunch, Louise cleared the table. "Say, how would you two like to have a big golden retriever?" she asked casually. Jeanne and I looked at each other with our mouths open. "Our daughter is moving, and she can't take him with her— Buckwheat is yours if you still want him."

"Want him?" Jeanne cried. She looked at me again. In my mind's eye I saw the three of us hiking the bog at sunset. I thought of cold winter nights with the three of us sitting close to the stove. I looked outside at the big dog prancing toward Jeanne. She held him close as he licked her face.

"He ought to make a good bogtrotter," Ted said.

37408515R00102

Made in the USA
Middletown, DE
30 November 2016